D1551571

RETHINKING

FORGIVENESS

Mental Tactics To Avoid Resentment

REVISED EDITION

Yvonne C. Hebert, MA

RETHINKING

FORGIVENESS

Mental Tactics to Avoid Resentment

Yvonne C. Hebert, MA

Books by Yvonne C. Hebert, M.A.

Finding Peace in Pain – 1984

Room for Another Heart – 2012
2nd Edition – Revised 2013

Rethinking Forgiveness – 2013
Mental Tactics to Avoid Resentment
Revised Edition - 2015

This book may be ordered through Amazon, on-line retailers, booksellers, and directly from the author at colliehouse@aol.com.
www.yvonnehebert.com

ISBN: 978-14929-10640
ISBN: 14929-10643

Library of Congress Control Number: TX 7-841-964
Printed in the United States of America

"To forgive is to set a prisoner free

And discover that the prisoner was you."

--Lewis B. Smedes, *"Forgive and Forget"*

Table of Contents

Dedication

This book is dedicated to my mother and grandmother

Sarah Jane (Jenny) Devlin

Ruth Ingalls

Acknowledgements

I would like to acknowledge the gracious support of the following people in the completion of this book.

Jonathon Dennis, DO, Sr. Ann Porter, OP, Marianne McDonald-Fisk, BSW, Laurilee Thompson-Flaugher, MEd, Rev. Alfonso Scott, Scott Smith, Kathy Box, and Karen Mackenroth, BA took their precious time to read the manuscript and point out areas that they believed needed attention.

All of these people were supportive of my efforts to look at forgiveness from a different perspective than is usually considered. Their encouragement and comments were very much appreciated and gave me the confidence to continue with this book.

Yvonne C. Hebert

April, 2015

Preface

Dear Reader:

Thank you for considering my book as your companion on a journey of enormous importance to your peace of mind.

As a therapist who has worked with hundreds of clients over my career, I believe that carrying resentment leads to a terrible cost in wasted life energies. Resentment deeply curtails the pleasures that people could be experiencing throughout their lives and infringes upon the lives of the people with whom they interact each day.

In searching for answers for myself and my clients, I found that most often forgiveness was held to a Biblical theme of finding the power to forgive through prayer and holding a Christian attitude toward forgiveness. I found that many of my clients were not only reluctant to embrace prayer as a means of finding forgiveness, they were sometimes outright hostile to the concept.

I believe that prayer can give the strength to survive incredible difficulties, even work miracles. But in the face of many of my clients' aversion to even the suggestion of prayer at such times, I had to not only find an explanation for this resistance, but also find a way to help them heal from their experience of perceived abuse.

Luckily, I remembered a World War I slogan which I had heard many times growing up: "Praise the Lord and Pass the Ammunition." I learned, and passed on to my clients, that while prayer is a powerful resource, it will not take the place of living in such a way as to avoid bitter feelings in the first place.

There are tactics an individual can learn to use which will prevent their feelings from being hurt in the first place. Utilizing these approaches to life events allows the individual to find peace from resentment and anger.

Over the years, I have come to believe that anger is like a muscle. The more you use it, the stronger it becomes and the more you depend on it to survive certain situations. I also believe that anger is hurtful to the individual and to those around them. The angrier a person is, the less able they are to enjoy the peace of mind that comes with being in control of themselves.

I know it's a tough world out there, and there are many abusive people and mean situations that are encountered daily. It is for that exact reason that I believe we need to be as free of anger and resentment as possible.

Anger clouds the mind. Encountering each new situation with a mind free of angry generalizations allows us to be at our wisest. Only then will we be in a position to get our desires met in situations or encounters with another person.

During our lifetimes we will encounter powers beyond our control which can, and do, harm us. To remain resentful only prolongs the damage which has been done to us. To remain resentful only adds to the many difficult moments in our lives that have left us with burdens difficult to dislodge from our hearts and minds.

I'm not suggesting that we become passive and let life just roll over us. I believe we need to be in such control of ourselves that we can be decisive and self-empowering even in difficult times. It isn't possible to be clear-thinking and purposeful if we've let a person or situation intimidate us emotionally.

This book deals with using our reason to understand ourselves and those around us. This gives us a choice in deciding if we are going to allow ourselves to be insulted by the words or behavior of others. Hopefully, I am also going to give my readers ammunition to forgive themselves for those situations they remember with regret.

After the publication of the first edition of this book, readers at my lectures told me about feelings they had to manage even after they were sure they had forgiven someone. I realized that while I had addressed this in the first edition, it was an area that needed much more clarification than I had given it. Accordingly I pulled the book from availability and rewrote the chapter on forgiving oneself. I hope this chapter now fully answers those concerns.

I would ask the reader to use this book as a workbook as often as possible. If the reader takes the time to answer the many questions detailed in this book, they will find themselves exploring their attitudes and thoughts as they read. Hopefully, this will lead to a better understanding of forgiveness and the role it plays in your life.

I hope this book brings positive change into your life and helps you have peaceful relationships with those around you.

Yvonne Hebert
April, 2015

"Not to forgive is to be imprisoned by the past,

By old grievances

That do not permit life to proceed with new business.

Not to forgive is to yield oneself to another's control...

To be locked into a sequence of act and response,

Of outrage and revenge, tit for tat, escalating always.

The present is endlessly overwhelmed and devoured by the past.

Forgiveness frees the forgiver.

It extracts the forgiver from someone else's nightmare."

--Lance Morrow, *The Chief: A Memoir of Fathers and Sons*

1

The Problem

"Hatred is blind, rage carries you away;
And he who pours out vengeance runs the risk
Of tasting a bitter draught."

--Alexander Dumas, *The Count of Monte Cristo*

Forgiving is hard. Whether you are trying to forgive yourself or someone else, it's still really hard. Forgiveness might be one of the most difficult challenges in life. Philosophers and teachers throughout the ages, and from every continent, have cautioned their followers to forgive others in order to live peacefully.

In the far distant past, Socrates had forgiveness in mind when he stated, "One should never do wrong in return, nor mistreat any man, no matter how one has been mistreated by him." The often-quoted wise man, Confucius, said "To be wronged is nothing, unless you continue to remember it." More recently, Nelson Mandela is quoted as saying" "Resentment is like drinking poison and then hoping it will kill your enemies."

The Bible is adamant on the subject, with the statement "Forgive that you may be forgiven." The Our Father Prayer says it just as clearly. "Forgive us our trespasses as we forgive those who trespass against us." Those are pretty daunting commands for a believer to hear who has felt betrayed and abused, and feels they have no recourse for amends.

One of the first things I would like to share with you is the need to be gentle with yourself. I think a cardinal rule in forgiving – yourself or someone else – is to be gentle with yourself. When we try to force ourselves to forgive other people, it becomes very hard work. It adds injury to insult. Someone has hurt us, we're upset about it and are told, "Forgive them" or "Forget it" and we can't.

That leads us to start thinking that something is wrong with us. We tell ourselves that other people must be able to do it or they wouldn't be so quick to tell us to forgive. So the first rule is to be gentle with yourself. Never try to force forgiveness.

Before we can contemplate an action like forgiveness, we need to fully understand what actually transpired. So our next step is to carefully consider what has happened to us – not just the surface encounter, but the deeper, emotional responses, as well as the ramifications of our reactions to the event.

Did the situation grow out of previous events where there were misunderstandings or hard feelings? Was it a deliberate affront to us or was it a careless or unwise remark? Could there have been another meaning to what was said or done? Was it a situation beyond our control?

Could we have altered the meanness of the event with a different response than we gave? What do we wish we had done or said? How would that have changed the impact on us and others? What significance did the event have for us?

Who else was involved? How did we affect other people because of our hurt feelings from that situation? How has it affected our day-to-day life? Has it changed us in some way? How are we going to bring this entire scenario with all of its ramifications to a stop?

Until we get some understanding of all the areas of our life that have been affected, it's very hard to even think of feeling peaceful about the event.

Learning to forgive can be the work of a lifetime. Many of us struggle with our feelings, reacting to them in times of stress. In addition, we often feel dissatisfied with our attempts to live in peace with ourselves and our neighbors.

When we understand that our reason can work effectively to help us maintain our peace of mind, we have gained a crucial insight into cultivating a sense of control over our emotional reactions in situations where we feel disrespected and angry.

We're born with a complex network of neurological and biological systems that work together to protect our bodies and minds from destruction. Some of these systems we intuitively understand and some we don't.

When we're hungry or thirsty, we know our bodies need nourishment to survive. So we eat and drink, trusting that our digestive system will turn the food and water into the elements our bodies need to feel strong again.

When we break a bone, we know we have injured our ability to move normally until the bone is healed. So we immobilize the injured area, trusting that the bone will grow together again.

When we learn to read and speak, we understand that we have found a way to communicate with other creatures. We use our abilities to converse with others and sure enough, they respond.

But some of our systems are hard to control or to understand. When another person treats us with what we perceive as disrespect, we feel an eruption of energy within us. Instinctively we want to protect ourselves, but often we can't act on this impulse. When we do try to defend ourselves, it can sometimes make the situation worse, which is even harder to understand.

When we enjoy the company of another person, we want to be around them often. But all too soon, this can become a nightmare of confusing feelings. Do they want to be with us? Do they like us as much as we like them? Can we trust them with our thoughts and feelings? If they do like us, why did they do something that made us feel betrayed? Why do they seem to be acting angry with us?

The question then becomes, "Where do these feelings come from?" Why aren't we just happy that the person is willing to spend time with us? Why do we want more reassurance from that person that we are likable? Why does their behavior make us question ourselves and ultimately the relationship?

While my answer may seem simplistic, I think it vibrates through every culture. As children, our security lies in pleasing our parents and siblings and later our teachers and classmates. To please all of these people, we must learn a complicated set of behaviors peculiar to our specific culture in a world of many different cultures.

Within our own community, there is the culture within our family which will be different from the family backgrounds of our neighbors. We could live next door to someone, be the same age, play together every day for years, and the psychological formation of each of us would still be evolving from many different customs.

Our parents brought their separate traditions together to create our immediate family's culture. We will have different ways of responding to situations, different ways of thinking about life and life events than any other family.

We will even use the same words differently. Certain words may not mean exactly the same to us as they do to our next door neighbors because of the diversities between the cultures of our families.

We're taught initially how to use words and what words mean within our nuclear family. Each of us uses our own very individual language when we talk. This word usage is formulated based on what our family taught us a word meant, our interpretation of how that word was used by others, or how that word was accepted by others when we used it.

We can never be absolutely sure that another person has understood exactly what we mean when we speak. This fact is particularly true if either of us is hearing the other's words through the dense screen of emotion.

When being understood is especially important to either party, a clarifying discussion about the subject is critical to be sure that everyone has heard and understood the meaning that each person has of the words used.

When we become aware that someone important to us seems to be nagging us about something or telling us the same story repeatedly, we can be absolutely sure that this person doesn't believe that we have understood what they were trying to share with us.

Such repetition is a sure indicator that a discussion is indicated and important. The speaker, having made repeated attempts to communicate their issue, may be too frustrated to suggest a conversation. They may have developed a feeling that the person they are trying to share with doesn't care about their feelings in that particular matter.

If we care about the relationship, it is vital that we make an effort to understand their position. To determine what they believe we do not comprehend, we should initiate a discussion to clarify their concerns.

A similar scenario should occur when someone feels insulted by another person. The insulted individual needs to initiate a thorough discussion if they wish to have clarity in the matter.

The other party may have no idea that their comment has been taken in a negative way by their companion. The insulted person may feel the first person was insensitive and abrasive, while the other person may believe they were being charming and funny.

There is an overlap of common behaviors and attitudes in relationships, but it's often difficult to know exactly where they are. This takes time and exposure to the other person through participating in different experiences, and by sharing our personal feelings and reactions before we gain a comfortable perspective on mutual similarities and differences.

The developing child must, eventually, leave the bosom of their family and enter the school system. They must learn the mores of the school they attend which will be similar to other schools in the area but not exactly the same. There will be subtle differences depending on the rules of each school, the family backgrounds of the many students, and the culture of that geographic area.

Additionally, our country will have specific values and behaviors which we must also learn. Our understandings of these customs are influenced by our friends, our church, and other organizations we attend. Political activities, television shows, movies, and advertising are only a few of the many powerful pressures we respond to daily. Understanding and absorbing all of these differing points in our specific culture is an enormous challenge for any child.

Each of us has a distinct personality based on heredity, family position, physical appearance, familial acceptance, medical history, and many other factors. Melding these variations of experiences and influences together makes each of us a unique individual.

As a unique individual, we will have different levels of anxiety or excitement in social events, and our approaches to humor almost certainly will differ. Various situations may make one person fearful while someone else won't even notice the incident. Such differences are clear to us early in life and make us sensitive to how well we are fitting into the social situations we encounter.

As adults we often hide our feelings of discomfort when we have concerns about not fitting in socially. Adults also have the freedom to choose whether or not they will participate in social gatherings where they feel uncomfortable. Even an adult's work life is often negotiable.

Children are less likely to be accepting of social differences and are forced into uncomfortable situations by parents or other influential adults. School, which children must attend, is an example of a stressful situation where they have little choice.

Aggressive children who are concerned about their own social acceptability will often bully other children with milder dispositions. It would seem that the teasing and assaults are intended to force the other child to behave in ways more like the bully or to make an example of the child with a gentler disposition.

While the bullied child may not be emotionally able to act like a bully, other children may adopt the bully's behavior patterns at school in an effort not to become targets themselves. If enough children begin to act more aggressively, the bully will feel more comfortable socially and won't have to make behavioral changes to ease their own pain and feelings of isolation.

This is true for the adult bullies in our world as well, whether in our circle of acquaintances, in the media, in corporate empires, or in government circles.

This bullying behavior is understandable. A child who changes a pattern of behavior learned at home while still living at home would incur the wrath of family members who do not appreciate the pressure this behavior change has placed on them.

Since security within the family is of paramount importance to a child, they will do what they have to do to maintain the family balance and still gain social acceptability among their peers.

Even as adults, we want to believe that our perception of the world we live in is correct. At the same time, we want to know that others approve of our views and that we fit into the social milieu surrounding us.

We spend a considerable amount of our time every day sharing our outlook on the world with our friends and co-workers. Our discussions can become quite lively at times as we talk about our lives, the behavior of celebrities, political leaders, current events, and the movies and shows we have seen.

Most folks have a close set of friends with whom they share their own thoughts and problems in dealing with others. Very often we find ourselves discussing the behavior of non-present friends which in some social circles may be considered poor form.

Gossip is generally considered a negative activity, but it can have a positive aspect. Gossip helps us determine what behaviors are acceptable in our social circle. It also lets us know when someone in our circle of friends needs support but is reticent to ask for it.

When we are discussing an issue where there is general acceptance, our conversation is relaxed and informative. As we begin talking about an issue where there is not general acceptance, our communication style changes to one that is livelier, perhaps punctuated with giggles or anger, depending on how each of us feels about the subject.

Material that we are not comfortable with, but with which we are consciously aware that we are ill at ease, such as sexual behaviors, will generally bring smiles, giggles, and even outright laughter. Such uncomfortable issues are often the basis of humor, and the stock-in-trade of the comedian.

Material that we do not allow our consciousness to accept as even remotely acceptable will bring tension, possibly anger, and even avoidance when these issues are broached to us. Such matters will be dispensed with quickly in most conversations.

Note that following such a discussion, participants will shift to very safe topics and will discuss them at length to avoid any further controversy. Among close friends where we feel emotionally very safe, we may talk about such topics a little longer. Note that in such a conversation, the tone of voice of the speakers is usually either very adamant or very questioning.

When someone violates our expectation of acceptable cultural conduct they have confronted us in this repressed area of our subconscious. When we feel insulted by whatever means our assailant takes, they are affecting us in those areas where we are the most sensitive and most unsure of ourselves. They have attacked our sense of personal dignity as a human being. Our concept of what constitutes our dignity is partially taught to us by the cultures we have lived in and partially by our very individual responses to our life experiences.

It is very difficult to forgive someone who has just under-valued us. It won't matter to us in that moment whether the person knew they were insulting us or not. When our social acceptability and personal worth is questioned, we feel provoked and in need of defending ourselves.

There is an axiom that knowledge is power, and that is certainly true in the case of insulting behavior. While one's emotional reaction will be instantaneous, the first step in forgiving is to spend some time reflecting upon the aggressing person's mental state before overtly responding.

A deliberate insult tells more about the aggressor than the victim. It speaks to the aggressor's need for power and control, and their lack of caring for the victim. It is helpful to understand that people who are often critical of other people are usually even more critical of, and angry with, themselves. Their critical behavior indicates a lack of confidence in their own social acceptability.

It is sometimes quite difficult to determine if offensive behavior is deliberate or unintentional. This is why taking the time to understand the motivation of the speaker is an essential step in avoiding resentments.

"Grudges are for those who insist that they are owed something;
Forgiveness, however, is for those
Who are substantial enough to move on."

--Criss Jami, *Salome': In Every Inch In Every Mile*

2

Why Forgiving Is So Hard To Do

"To Forgive Does Not Mean to Condone"

--Allan Lokos, *Patience, The Art of Peaceful Living*

I clearly remember a devastating moment in my childhood when I found myself confronted by a school friend's betrayal and the crushing hurt that burned in my young heart so hotly that I knew I would never forget nor forgive.

I came home from school in tears. My very best friend had picked a classmate over me for her lunch companion, completely ignoring me, and I was devastated. We had lunched together every school day for four years, told each other our secrets, and shared our problems and triumphs.

Today, without a word, she walked past me with a new friend as if she didn't know me. I held it together long enough to go through classes at school that afternoon. But my heart was deeply wounded and walking home that afternoon, the tears had started.

"What happened to you?" my mother exclaimed when she saw me.

She listened quietly to my 10-year-old explanation of this terrible treachery and offered the usual consolations, but her words did nothing to heal the hurt.

"You need to forgive her and move on," my mother said finally.

"I'll never forgive her," I sputtered through my tears. "She was mean."

"You're old enough to understand something," my mother spoke quietly. "Not forgiving her is hurting you, not her. My mother told me something I'm going to pass on to you. I don't want you to forget it."

My ears perked up, and my tears slowed. This must be really important information. I had never met my grandmother, deceased long before I was born.

"If you really want to hurt someone," my mother continued, "make them really angry at you and then forget them. They'll suffer all their lives with those hurt feelings because people have a very hard time forgiving others."

"I don't understand," I said, my forehead furrowed with the strain of trying to understand this weird concept.

"Someday you will," she said. "In the meantime, if you must stay angry at your friend, you'll just have to suffer."

It took me thirty years and two degrees in clinical psychology before I finally understood what my mother had tried to tell me that afternoon.

Forgiveness isn't letting the other person off the hook for what they have done or said. It's taking you off the hook and putting the responsibility for the situation squarely on the shoulders of the person who created it.

This is a concept that everyone needs to understand. Forgiving isn't for the other person. Forgiving is for you. Whether you forgive your aggressor or not means nothing to them. They are going right ahead with their lives.

In most instances, they don't even know you're not forgiving them for something. They couldn't care less. Their lives are going on. You're the one who is nursing the upset stomach. You're the one that's grinding about it all the time. You're the one who is wondering how to get even.

It's not going to matter to the other person if you forgive them or not. Many people won't even know they did anything to upset you. They don't even know they need forgiving. You need to make the decision to forgive them even though they don't deserve it, because you do deserve to live in peace.

It's also important to recognize that your feelings are your responsibility. You do not have to be hurt or offended by what any-one says or does. That is a choice you make. It is your willingness to accept the other person's treatment of you as valid or invalid that determines whether you will be resentful or amused by their action.

If someone has made an unkind remark about you, or given a negative appraisal of you or something you have done, why are you giving it credence? Do you believe they are right?

If you do, why are you upset? If it is who you are, if it is something that you have done, then you chose to be or do what they are criticizing. You have every right to be, or do, what they don't like. That is your choice and yours alone to make.

Perhaps they have made a negative comment about something you don't like about yourself, or maybe an action that you wish you hadn't taken. In that case their criticism has brought attention to something that you have the power to change.

If you don't want to change, that is your choice and you have the right to make that choice. You have the right to be exactly who you are whether others like you that way or not.

If their statement is not the truth about you, what is causing your pain? Are you angry because they are misrepresenting something about you? Are you concerned that someone else will believe what they have said? How will it affect you if someone you don't know listens to a negative statement about you?

Question yourself about the character of a person who would believe negative remarks about a person they didn't know. If you don't know them, and you never meet them in the future, why do you care what they think about you?

If you do someday meet them, can you believe that their opinion of you will change as they get to know you? Will they even remember what their friend once told them about you?

Another point to consider is the very real possibility that the person making an untrue statement about you may often make irresponsible or negative remarks about other people as well. It's doubtful that a responsible person will be likely to give credence to statements made by such a person.

Another possibly is the realization that the speaker may actually believe that you do not measure up to their standards of behavior. The question then becomes, why do you care so much what this other person thinks of you? Who are they to you? Why is this person's opinion so important to you that you are letting them control your emotions and perhaps even your behavior?

Are they enjoying a lifestyle that you would like to share? Do they evidence attitudes you would like to adopt into your own life? Are you afraid of losing them as a friend or lover?

Do they occupy an influential position in your life such as an employer or a friend of a close friend? Are they a classmate who can impact your acceptance by other classmates? Are they a co-worker who can affect your position and/or acceptance on your job?

How powerful a position do they play in your life? Do you need to keep them in your life? How would your life change if they were to disappear from your life? Ask yourself honestly: why are they in your life? What do you want from them?

"Fool that I am," said he, "that I did not tear out my heart
The day I resolved to revenge myself."

--Alexander Dumas, *The Count of Monte Cristo*

3

Types of People in Our Lives

"Before we can forgive one another,
We have to understand one another."

--Emma Goldman

It took years of working on my own hurts as well as working with
other people suffering through bouts of anger and depression before
I sorted out some answers. Many years ago I finally decided that
there are four types of people in this world. It depends on the kind
of person with whom you are interacting as to how you can best
respond to them.

It should be pointed out that any of us can be Type #1 some of the time and Type #2 with other issues. That's probably where many of us are. Our own needs get in the way of our being as open and caring as we would like to be. We may also move from group to group depending on the person with whom we are interacting.

Type #1 is a responsible, reasonable person with the usual human idiosyncrasies that make them charming, lovable and sometimes annoying.

Type #2 is a person with qualities that we enjoy and may be drawn to but because of their own emotional conflicts they are unable to be responsive in all of their behaviors. We may find that they are not reliable as friends in a few, or perhaps many, areas of life.

Type #3 is a person that feels justified in hurting other people. They may demand to control other people, or deliberately focus harsh attention on what they perceive as weaknesses in other folks. They may be physically, mentally, and/or emotionally abusive to others.

Type #4 is the person disabled by an emotional illness that deprives them of the capacity to be aware of the effect of their words and behavior on others.

Let's explore in greater depth these various types of people and how to tell them apart, as well as how to respond to each of them.

Type #1

The Type #1 person is basically conscientious, at peace with them-selves, and means well toward other people. You enjoy their company generally and they seem aware of you and your needs most of the time. If they say they will do something, bar an emergency, they will do it. However, on occasion, they may say or do something that you find painful or offensive.

Your first step is to let them know how you perceived their behavior toward you. Tell them what those words or actions meant to you and how they made you feel. You'll know from their response how to treat them in the future.

If they say "Oh, I didn't mean it like that!" and then explain what they did mean and apologize for the misunderstanding, give them another chance. Keep trust in the relationship.

This is the perfect opportunity for both of you to gain a deeper understanding of each other. Having an open, calm, and rational discussion of both of your needs as they relate to the situation can bring a closer, stronger bond between you.

Having such a discussion with another person may help us take a different look at the situation. As you look at the various aspects of the event, you may begin to recognize that the hurt didn't come so much from the other person as from inside yourself. Your memories of upsetting experiences in the past have made you sensitive to particular words and behaviors. Your friend didn't hurt you intentionally. They didn't know your past history.

Jim and Jenny, a young couple who had been married just three years came to my office in deep distress one summer. Jenny had asked Jim for a divorce and he was deeply opposed to separating from her.

"He won't call when he knows he's going to be late coming home from work," Jenny explained. "That doesn't sound like a big deal, I guess, but I'm frantic wondering what has happened to him. When he does get home, I'm hysterical, and he thinks I'm crazy for being upset."

"I don't work late that often," Jim asserted. "It's just once in a while and she knows I'm coming home. I would never cheat on her. I've loved her since the 10th grade. I want to be at home with her, but sometimes things happen and I'm late."

"I believe he wouldn't cheat on me," she said, tears welling in her eyes, "but I can imagine all kinds of things happening to him. And dinner is always ruined. If I knew he was going to be an hour late, I'd start dinner later. He just won't call."

As we discussed the problem that had wedged between them, it soon became evident that Jim had, on occasion, worked almost three hours overtime without calling home. He said that he felt the need to work as hard as his employer asked so that he could provide well for his wife and their future family. He couldn't understand why she didn't understand this.

Jim's patience began to wear thin under the accusations she was making, and he finally stated that he felt like a little boy who had to account for all of his time.

"It feels like I'm living with my mother again," he declared bitterly. "I'm a grown man and I know my responsibilities. I don't need someone constantly checking on me. I can find my way home without any help."

"That's not the point," Jenny wailed.

"Well, it is to me," Jim asserted, somewhat defiantly.

That was the opening for which I had been waiting. There had finally been a clear statement that they were both looking at the situation from the standpoint of different needs. Further discussion centered on these separate perspectives.

Jim had been raised in a home where he had to account for every minute of his time, and had yearned for the days when he could come and go as he pleased. He felt smothered by parents who took him to school and picked him up afterwards, gave him an allowance but told him what to do with much of it, picked out his clothes, and shared almost every meal together. To some people, this would have been a stable, integrated family but to Jim it was stifling.

Jenny had been raised in a family where the members shared some family activities and valued their time together, but in a more casual manner. Unlike Jim, she was given an allowance with no strings attached other than it was a limited amount. If she wanted something special, she had to save for it or do without. While her family did not pick out her clothes, they were free with their opinions about the way family members dressed which was sometimes hurtful.

Family members were active in many outside activities and rarely had the time to attend each other's activities as a family. Except for Sunday, it was rare for everyone to be in attendance at a meal which were often "pick-up" meals. Each person scrawled their schedule on a chalkboard in the kitchen. Everyone, even the parents, kept to a curfew when they could be counted on to be home.

While Jim saw Jenny's need to know when he was getting home as regulation of his activities, Jenny saw it as giving her the time to do other things while waiting for him to join her.

"I work too," she commented. "I have a lot of things to do to keep the house running. If I knew he was going to be an hour or so late getting home, I could takes clothes to the cleaners, or do some shopping, or visit a friend. It would free up our weekends a little. But by the time I know he isn't showing up, I have dinner ready, and there's nothing to do but wait because I don't know if he's going to be home in twenty minutes or two hours.

"Not to mention," she added, a little wearily, "that I've become anxious and worried that he might have been in an accident and not been able to let me know. I can't imagine how he can say that he loves me and then let me worry about him for hours."

"I kind of like it when I see she's worried about me," Jim admitted sheepishly. "I know then that she really misses me and loves me."

"And that," Jenny pointed out bitterly, "is exactly why I want to leave him. He tortures me with worry to make himself feel good. I don't want to hurt like that anymore."

Jim, shocked by this statement from Jennie, reached out to her immediately. He moved closer to her on the couch and grasped her hands in his.

"I don't want to hurt you," he exclaimed. "I didn't know that's what you thought I meant. I just meant I love to see you happy to see me."

"That's not what you said," she retorted.

"Then I said it wrong," he apologized.

I learned that both of them had said these things to each other in the past, but never when they were in a frame of mind to hear the meaning of what the other was saying.

When he heard Jenny's position in a non-threatening dialog, Jim was able to make the decision that her needs in this matter outweighed his need for independence. He promised to call home if he was going to be late. Jennie decided that she could call him before starting supper to be sure that he was on his way home. They also agreed on two nights a week when Jennie would not fix dinner and neither of them would need to come directly home from work.

Out of their very different backgrounds, they formed a new tradition for their family. Interestingly, I learned later that neither of them had made use of the two free nights each week. They found themselves talking at the end of their workday by phone and often going out together for dinner or some other form of entertainment.

While Jim felt stifled with the requirement that he report his schedule to his wife, he welcomed her call to him each evening as an indication of her caring for him and wanting to be with him. He felt appreciated. Coming home on time every evening made him feel that he was the only one making an effort to be together as a family. While Jenny could argue that point, she also felt that making a phone call every evening was not a big deal if he needed it to feel loved.

Their situation had triggered memories of the past where they had learned to have expectations, some positive and some negative. They had entered an adult relationship without resolving the painful aspects of their childhood family relationships.

This is a truth for all of us. Current situations can trigger recollections from the past when you felt abused and the situations were never healed in your mind. If you did not have these difficult memories you might never have been upset by a careless comment from someone.

Another person can say or do anything. It doesn't need to affect us in a negative way. It does affect us when we put current situations into the context of the past.

The better you get to know yourself, the less anybody can bother you. The more you become responsible for your own behavior and are comfortable with your own self, the less another person can disturb your peace.

Being sensitive to the other person's needs is crucial in any kind of personal conversation. They may be finding it difficult to have a discussion with you. Their insides may be reeling with the information you have already shared with them. The other person may need time to recover emotionally and think about what the conversation has meant to them.

Share that you are willing to discuss the situation again if that is their desire. Be sure to let them know if you come to the realization that it was your history, not them, that caused your discomfort.

Keep in mind that an apology is only as good as one's future actions. If another person can be believed in this area of your life there won't be repeats of the particular type of transgression you have discussed as insulting or painful. Your friend will remember that this is an area where you are sensitive and will be careful to avoid repeating those words or actions around you. As you go through your life with this friend, there may well be other situations where you are offended and need to speak up.

Your friend may even recognize that the behavior that offended you would be offensive to other people as well. Your friend might do the necessary personal growing to modify the way they interact with other people generally.

Keep in mind that as your relationship builds, you will also be doing some apologizing and making some behavior changes to avoid offending your friend. It's a two-way street. If you expect understanding from your friends, it will be important to remember that you have to be just as aware of their needs and feelings.

"A broken friendship that is mended through forgiveness
Can be even stronger than it once was."

--Stephen Richards,

Forgiveness and Love Conquers All: Healing the Emotional Self

Type #2

The Type #2 person may seem like the person described above. They say, "Oh, I'm sorry, I didn't know..." but in time the behavior occurs again or the words are spoken again. Again you bring it to their attention, and, possibly acting embarrassed, they laugh it off with another apology.

Now it's decision time for you. It's time to think about the relationship in a very serious manner. How important is this person to you? Is this a business relationship where you must interact with them? Is this a personal relationship where you feel unable to detach yourself? Or is this a relationship where you can release the person and move on to spend your time and energy with people who are ready to establish a more responsible friendship?

The first step is to recognize that this person is unlikely to change their ways and it probably has nothing to do with you.

It's important to place responsibility for their behavior with them. It may be that you could talk with them for days and they would never understand what you were upset about. The situation covers an area where they are too bound by the past, too hurt themselves, to acknowledge an understanding.

So the question becomes: "Is it worth going through uncomfortable or hurtful situations periodically just to know this person?" If you decide that for whatever reason you are going to continue to relate to this person, it's imperative that you protect your feelings around them. In whatever way this friend is unable to modify their desire to control others or is unaware of their offensive behavior, take the responsibility for avoiding such situations.

Some examples:

Don't tell secrets to someone who won't keep them.

Avoid making social plans for anything important to you with someone who persists in wanting to control or change the details as the date of the event nears.

Don't loan money or items to someone who forgets their obligations.

In the work world, keep very accurate documentation of all interactions with them so you can defend yourself if necessary.

I once had a friend, older than myself and an ex-actress, who was always late. In many other ways she was a dependable and fun friend. I decided that the relationship was worth accommodating her need to make a 'Grand Entrance.'

But I also changed my behaviors with her. Since she was always twenty minutes to a half hour late, I stopped arriving on time and assumed an appointment time fifteen-plus minutes later than we agreed on. I still had to wait for her a few minutes but not so long as to make me angry with her. I also took responsibility for my decision to accommodate her not-so-charming behavioral foible.

When time was important to me, I arranged to meet at her home. In this way I was able to cut down the distractions that would entice her to be late. Since I was making the entrance by going to her home, she was able to play the 'Gracious Hostess.'

I also stopped meeting her if getting to an event on time was important to me. Instead, I went with other friends and let her meet us there.

I wouldn't have made these accommodations with many other people, but I enjoyed her company. She was a good-hearted woman, funny and entertaining. She was also tolerant of some of my onerous behaviors. It was definitely a two-way street.

"The stupid neither forgive nor forget;
The naïve forgive and forget;
The wise forgive but do not forget."

--Thomas Stephen Szasz

Type #3

Type #3 are individuals who inflict an inordinate amount of control on other people and situations. While they seem to be spirited people who know what they want from life, a long-term relationship with them can become difficult for a person of more moderate temperament. Institutions and employers, as well as individuals, can fit into this category.

This abusive personality is often encountered in our culture and even encouraged by our media and business practices. But it is a type that causes considerable hardship to other people. It is almost impossible to avoid such people either at work or within families. Therefore, we will look at this type from differing perspectives.

Identifying Type #3

You'll know Type #3 through observation of their behaviors over time. In addition to their need to be controlling, they may engage in considerable negative gossip about other people. They probably will demonstrate a critical derision of the human failings of other people – often times within earshot of the person they are putting down. They generally treat animals in a careless or inhumane manner. You may notice that such people often scream in anger and frustration at their children and other family members.

Type #3 has a strong tendency to monopolize the people they are able to control and to slowly curtail their access to other friends and family. Over time, a person in such a relationship may realize that they have been effectively isolated from other people.

These individuals are often charming when you first meet them. They draw people to them like flies to honey. So if, by chance, you fail to notice red flags in the early stages of your relationship with them, understand that it takes time to get to know another person.

These people are often very adept at attracting people to themselves, camouflaging their need for control, and re-writing history when they are cornered by facts. They are also masters at sizing up the weaknesses of other people and learning how to manipulate them for their own benefit.

Don't beat yourself up when you suddenly find yourself a target and see the triumphant, angry glow in their eyes. There will be no apologies here. You will be told in no uncertain terms that you are too sensitive, or you deserved what you got, or they were defending themselves from you. If at all possible, chalk this relationship up to experience and find the nearest door.

Keep in mind that they, like you, have every right to be whatever kind of person they choose to be. But behaviors have consequences and carry with them responsibilities. So they are choosing to be responsible for the consequences of their behavior.

Some abusive people have a painful history and have lost their ability to trust other people. They often function on the premise that if they don't control situations in which they find themselves, their needs will not be met.

Is it possible for a controlling, manipulative person to change and become a person that doesn't harm the people around them? It is. Everyone can change, but they have to want to become a more trusting and responsive friend to other people.

Considerations Relative to Leaving the Relationship

People who enjoy hurting other people are people to avoid. When you find yourself participating in a friendship, or a more complicated relationship, with an individual whose behavior choices are causing you pain, it's time to search for the answers to two questions.

1. Is the individual capable of change?
2. Can you leave the relationship?

Confronting an abusive individual is not easy and requires a 'tread lightly' approach. Letting them know that you care about the relationship with them but that you are uncomfortable with some of the situations the two of you have been through might be a good place to start. An individual that becomes volatile in such a conversation is giving you the information you need to recognize that a trusting relationship is not possible with them.

If they are willing to have the conversation, let them know how they are affecting other people. Usually people's behavioral patterns become solidly set in childhood and they don't fully realize how they are appearing to other people or that they are hurting the people around them. An honest talk may give them a chance to make the decision to change. Depending on the strength of their abusive patterns, they may be able to make such changes on their own through the use of self-help books, revealing talks with relatives and friends, and other such tools.

The probability, however, is that they have chosen their character path out of deep fears, painful memories, and childhood training and will need the assistance of a skilled psychotherapist at least for a time.

It may also become very clear that they have no intention of making the effort to become a person more sensitive to the people around them. They may really like who they are or not be able to imagine themselves coping with life successfully being less critical and controlling than they are.

If this latter scenario is the one that you encounter, there is a need for you to take a serious look at the ramifications of continuing your relationship with a person who relies on skillful manipulation, criticism, and control of others to make their way through life.

Why Should You Leave the Relationship if You are Able?

Abusive people are toxic to the people around them. The longer you are in the relationship, the more toxic it becomes. For an individual to be dependent upon an abusive person is even more destructive since the dependent person eventually perceives themselves as helpless to protect themselves from harm.

When treated badly by a manipulative person, the victim has a natural reaction to want to get even. An abusive type of person seems to kindle a fire in their victims for revenge. There is a deep consciousness of betrayal that the victim feels since the abuser has been so charming in the past.

When the abuser shows their true colors, part of the emotional devastation that the victim feels is the knowledge that the relationship has been based on deceit.

The relationship then becomes a battle for control which the victim can only win by refusing to play the game. The abuser holds the best cards since they have gotten to know the victim well and have kept their own weaknesses hidden. Additionally, the victim is seldom skilled at manipulative behavior. Until the abused person exits this unfortunate liaison, they will continue to be abused.

Unfortunately, many marriages slide into this never-ending battle for ego-saving control. It's a lose-lose game. There's no way to even the score, no matter how the game got started.

Some abusers become very penitent, particularly after a physical assault on another person. The victim starts to feel mollified and then enjoys the position of being catered to in some way. Their bruised body and emotions begin to mend. They feel a sense of power having such a powerful-acting person as the abuser showing concern and caring for them. In keeping with their own temperament, they try to forgive and forget and hope the situation won't re-occur.

The bitter truth is, however, that no one can be an innocent victim twice. The first time the responsibility belongs to the aggressor. After that, you've agreed to be the punching bag. The old adage "Fool me once, shame on you. Fool me twice, shame on me," applies here.

If you can leave a relationship with an abusive individual and you choose to stay, it's time to ask yourself some painful questions about your own emotional needs. Obtain whatever support you need, professional or lay, to heal your willingness to tolerate abusive behavior of any kind from any person.

When there are children involved, it is even more important that such behavior in the home be brought to a halt. Children learn what they see and what they live. Children subjected to abuse learn to be abusive to others. They learn to disrespect other people and authorities. Or they learn that they have no self-worth and live their lives as victims. Either way, they are being led into unhappy lives with frustrating relationships.

People need to make every effort to insist on family or couple therapy to confront abusive behavior patterns in the home. Sometimes both parents are abusive in different ways and only see the abusive behaviors of their partner. Over time, a therapist will be able to discern this pattern and confront it for the healing of both parties.

The cardinal rule to know about abusers is that their behavior can, and usually does, escalate. It may start with mental or emotional abuse. It usually advances to physical assaults that can intensify to the point of lethality.

Abusers do not feel safe unless they have control of every person and every situation in their world. When an abuser has found someone who tolerates their manipulative behavior, they do become dependent on that person.

When the victim walks away from the situation, literally or figuratively, the abuser feels out of control. This is a feeling they have fought all their life. It makes them feel helpless, and helplessness is terrifying to them. To cover this feeling of deep pain, they become angry and some of these people can become quite dangerous.

When the victim leaves such a relationship, it is natural for them to feel emotional about the decision, even ambivalent. When faced with the anger and hurt expressed by their abusive partner, many people become confused and return to the situation.

If you find yourself in this predicament, think carefully about what the best decision is that you can make for yourself, not the other person. Victims have been made to feel that they have no value, or that they are selfish, and they have difficulty giving their own needs the dominant position in their decision-making process.

Don't waste your time in resentment or trying to get even. It is false reasoning to think that your behavior is causing the other person to become abusive. Believing that you need their protection, or that you haven't loved them enough, is pure romantic fiction. Without effective intervention an abuser will be abusive no matter how another person behaves.

When You Feel You Can't Leave the Relationship

There are many reasons why an individual can become trapped in an abusive situation from which they do not feel they can extricate themselves. Some situations which I have been aware of include:

- An elderly person married to an alcoholic, abusive partner was unable to obtain the financial support from the community to move to a more life-giving environment.
- A disabled person, dependent upon an abusive parent was unable to obtain necessary support to live in a different environment.
- An elderly person, physically afraid of a drug-using child who regularly demanded their money or possessions, was not able to protect themselves from the child, even with legal injunctions.

- An adult child of an abusive parent felt they had little recourse but to help the parent in the parent's last years.

- The spouse of a controlling individual held deep convictions about the permanency of marriage and the effect separation would have on their children and even their extended family. This spouse only left the relationship when they were convinced the partner was having extramarital affairs.

- Abusive partners of adult siblings are a part of family gatherings. The children of such marriages may also be difficult persons and they are part of the life of an extended family.

- Critical, perfectionistic managers who demean employees are legendary. Employers are noted for many kinds of abuse directed at people working under their supervision.

- And, of course, there is the incarcerated individual who feels humiliated and over-powered.

Later in this book is a chapter on *"Protecting Yourself"* from abusers. People caught in these situations should employ as many of these tools as practical in their particular circumstance.

As an on-going, defensive tool against the abusers in our life, an individual needs to find emotional support. As pointed out earlier, abusers often isolate their victims from family and friends so that regular support is difficult. However there are crisis centers and hospitals with counseling care available if the victim has access to a telephone.

If you know of someone living in difficult circumstances, it is important to extend support in whatever way the person is able to accept. Very often just listening to this person talk is the greatest kindness you can offer to them.

An abused person becomes isolated within themselves, as well as from other people. They have a desperate need to share their ordeal but also feel that no one will believe or understand what they are experiencing.

Many people think that they need to solve the other person's problem, so they offer advice. This is usually counterproductive since the person offering advice never knows the victim's entire story. If a person is allowed to talk without criticism or advice, they will usually find their own truth and their own solutions.

Words can rarely convey the entire experience with which a person is coping, so advice seldom fits their circumstances adequately enough for them to follow it. The unfortunate result is that the person offering advice feels unappreciated for their caring and interest. The afflicted individual feels uncomfortable sharing their feelings since they can't seem to make others understand the reality of what is happening to them.

The best tactic is to let such an individual talk freely and to keep their confidences inviolate so they will feel free to share with you again. Make them aware of safe houses in the area, professional counseling that could be available to them if they wanted it, and other resources, but make it clear you don't know what's best for them to do. If you realize their life is in danger, contact appropriate authorities for guidance.

While most cases of physical assault are made by men against their women, the opposite situation does occur more often than society wants to believe.

Men with abusive wives rarely ask for help with this problem because they believe that, as men, they should be able to protect themselves. They are deeply embarrassed that they are tolerating assaults and ashamed to ask for help. They are often aware that their children are also suffering abuse, especially when they are not at home to intervene.

Yet the men I have talked with who were in this situation are deeply in need of support and guidance for themselves and for their children. Professional therapists and counselors are trained to help men as well as women in abusive relationships. The staff in many women's shelters are also trained to work with both women and men.

For people going through these very difficult situations, forgiveness becomes extremely difficult. Resentment, depression, anxiety and isolation become a lifestyle that affects the health and well-being of these individuals.

The individuals in these situations need to take the time to learn how to protect themselves from the pathology of the angry people in their lives. The chapter on *"Protecting Yourself"* will give them some tools with which to start.

But most importantly, they need to develop a support system away from the toxic situation they can't leave. Even if this support is entirely by phone, it is important for them to reach out and ask for positive reinforcement from other people or agencies. They should not try to endure the pain of their life in isolation.

For those able to leave their home, craft classes where they can be creative and feel the positive energy of other creative people is richly beneficial to their spirit. Involving themselves in any activity that they find relaxing, fun, and inspiring is helpful.

Learning to ignore, as much as possible, the underlying messages in the comments made by the controlling people with whom they are associated is a very effective tactic. Learn to let the barbs roll over you without penetrating your sense of personal dignity.

Keep in mind that not responding to a comment doesn't mean you agree with it. Know that you don't have to react to caustic or sarcastic remarks, no matter who makes them. You don't have to answer an intrusive question directed at you, or otherwise allow yourself to be baited into an argument that you don't want to have.

Always keep in mind that your safety is first. When you cannot leave an abusive situation, it may be wiser to re-assure an abusive person of their power rather than to confront it alone.

One last thought for those living or working in abusive situations – keep your energies focused away from those individuals who would control your life. If you love an abusive person, enjoy the good times, but disengage your energies when they start being mean.

Focus your energy on those people you love who are loving, on those activities which give you inspiration and strength, and on the thoughts that bring you peace.

Remember that life has a learning curve. You'll be wiser when you meet the next abuser, and you will meet another such person. The world is full of abusers.

"As I walked out the door toward the gate
That would lead to my freedom,
I knew if I didn't leave my bitterness and hatred behind,
I'd still be in prison."

--Nelson Mandela

Type #4

The emotionally distressed individual can be very hurtful to others without ever meaning to be. They are so wrapped up in their own world that often times other people are not entirely real to them. Their own feelings are often incapacitating. Other emotions may surface as a defense to protect them from these deeper painful feelings.

This disconnectedness between what they are feeling, and how they are acting, leaves them confused, frustrated, and sometimes offensive to others. Additionally, their emotional illness can leave them very sensitive to being offended by other people. This leaves them feeling anger and resentment which they may find difficult to hide. Without a clear understanding of their own feelings, they often act out behaviorally.

Medications can be a great help to folks in this situation, but can create other problems for the individual. They may make the person more stable emotionally, but feeling nauseous much of the time. They may have muscle aches or headaches. Even the constant dry mouth associated with some medications can interfere with a person's ability to communicate well.

Even when their mood is reasonably stable, they may have serious doubts about how they are being perceived by others or if their behavior is entirely appropriate.

Feeling hurt by their words or behavior is to misunderstand the situation. These people are rarely able to recognize that they have hurt other folks, but many of them would care if they knew.

It may be that there are situations or times when they are able to be open and free and to communicate well. Enjoy those times but be prepared to protect yourself if needed.

When you find yourself offended by persons of this type, take a deep breath, and do a reality check. Recognize that whatever happened has very little, if anything, to do with you.

Don't expect a peer relationship with this person, at least not during acute phases of their condition. It's a kindness to offer support and concern if you can do that without having expectations of constant reliable behavior from them.

Such folks do, on occasion, surprise others with keen perceptiveness and understanding. Family members and caring friends could maintain their relationship as a support to the person during the tough times, and to enjoy the good days.

"When you are depressed, you need the love of other people,
And yet depression fosters actions that destroy that love.
Depressed people often stick pins into their own life rafts.
The conscious mind can intervene. One is not helpless."

--Andrew Soloman, *The Noonday Demon: An Atlas of Depression*

"Forgiveness in no way requires
That you trust the one you forgive."

--William Paul Young, *The Shack*

4

Implications of Forgiveness

"Forgiving is not an occasional act,
It is a constant attitude."

--Martin Luther King, Jr.

Forgiveness implies a willingness to let the other person be whoever they are, with no strings attached. We give them the right to be tolerant or manipulative, as they wish. We allow them to take the full responsibility for their words, their actions, and their point of view of life. We give them the right to think whatever they wish about us, about events, about what is socially acceptable and what is not.

Forgiving also implies that we have these same rights to be whoever we are without apology or explanation. Forgiving also means that with these rights comes the assumption of responsibility for the consequences of the behaviors and the words which each of us have chosen. The consequences of our behaviors and words extend far beyond those people in our immediate vicinity.

Consider what happens when we drop a rock in a pool of water. The ripples from the rock splashing into the water roll farther and farther away from the point of impact – but they started with the rock falling into the water. So it is with our behavior and words. Our responsibility for our words and behavior extends not only to those people directly affected by us but also to those who are indirectly influenced because of the way we have impacted the emotions of others.

The Anger Response

When we do not live with forgiveness as a habit, our usual response to an offense, real or imagined, is to become angry. This anger is actually an emotional defense that allows us to not recognize the deep emotions that surge within us.

Our anger demands that the other person make amends to us and when they don't, we feel even more anger. There are several facets to anger which, if understood, are helpful in forgiving others.

Anger as an Emotional Defense

First of all, as mentioned earlier, our anger is a screen to cover our own deep feelings of hurt, fear and/or rejection. It is helpful to look at what these angry feelings might actually mean to us.

- Is it possible that we are afraid that if we confront the person who has angered us, they will be offended and abandon us?

- Does this possibility make us fear that we will then be alone, without the anchor that person has represented in our life?

- Are we afraid that we will never find another person to fill the gap left by the loss of that friend?

- Do we believe that we actually are unlovable, or in some way unacceptable to others?

- Are we afraid that if we confront this person, such hostility will be provoked in one or both individuals that someone could get physically hurt or the situation could explode to become even worse?

- If we have been physically assaulted by another person, are we feeling helpless and unable to protect ourselves in the future?

- Are we feeling that no one will believe our innocence in a physical assault?

- Are we feeling there is no way for us to achieve any form of justice for a physical assault or other form of wrong done to us?

It's very important that we take a fearless look at our emotions and what we are feeling deep inside our souls. Without a clear knowledge of the damage done to our psyche, repairing the harm becomes very difficult, if not impossible.

Generalizing Resentment

Our anger continues to be stoked by our need to force an apology from the offending party. When it isn't forthcoming, or the apology offered is not deemed sincere, our anger can settle into a smoldering resentment.

Such resentments can generalize over time and extend to other people who remind us of the offending person, or to situations similar to the one where we felt distressed.

In time, without ever being overtly conscious of our change in behavior we may find ourselves avoiding certain social situations. We may even find ourselves avoiding people who look or act in ways that remind us of our resentment.

We may find ourselves reacting with impatience, even anger to innocent individuals who have the misfortune to remind us of a person toward whom we feel resentment.

We do this automatically, without conscious choice. We are emotionally desperate to avoid the anger, the bitterness, the hurt that overtakes us when our subconscious recognizes this similarity to the past. This effort to avoid resentment can change our life forever.

Directed Anger

The next facet of anger to consider is where we direct that anger which is often to the person who has offended us.

We need to fully understand that our demand for amends is an effort to control the person who has hurt us. We want to force them to behave in a manner that we believe is socially acceptable.

We need them to recognize what a worthy person we are. We need them to be sorry that they have disrespected us, embarrassed us in front of other people, or otherwise exploited us.

No one can force another person to regret their behavior. Apologies must be freely given and acted out through a change of conduct. Without this change, an apology is meaningless and our emotional response will continue to be resentful, even if we initially accept the apology.

Maturing Adequately to Accept Change

The emotional maturation required for sincere apologies and the ability to change only happen with a personal awareness which develops over a long time in most individuals. With careful guidance from parents and teachers, such maturity can develop during our growing up years. For many people however, life events interfere, and emotional maturity continues to develop during their adult years.

Efforts to change require great energy and concentration. Without full commitment and understanding of the need for change, we are destined to fail.

Waiting for another person to mature emotionally in some area and change their ways before you allow yourself to find peace of mind is risking your own happiness for a very long time – perhaps your entire lifetime! Waiting for emotional change in another person is placing your emotional freedom in the hands of the enemy, or at best, a person who does not recognize the impact of their behavior on your emotional life.

If an offensive person resists your efforts to bring them to an awareness of how they have impacted you, chalk the injury up to experience and move on with your life.

Misdirected Anger

Rather often in life, we see someone angry with one person take out their anger on another innocent person. There can be many reasons for this.

They may not have been able to show their anger to someone they considered too powerful to confront directly, or they may be angry with someone of whom they are physically afraid.

They may not want to deal with the repercussions of letting someone they love know how angry they are.

They may have been confused at their own reaction at the moment they took offense, rendering them verbally powerless and missed the moment to confront the person who angered them.

We often see drivers who respond with anger to someone in their own car when they are unable to communicate with another driver who has offended them.

Unbelievable as this may seem, people will sometimes focus their anger on another person when they cannot accept the reality of their own behavior. As an actual fact they may be deeply upset with themselves but unable at the moment to process this information. If they are a person who is in the habit of reacting to inner turmoil with anger, they will probably strike out at whoever is close at hand.

Whoever in their life or whatever the situation may have been which stimulated their anger, spouses, children, and pets often get the brunt of misdirected anger.

The recipient of misdirected anger is rightfully confused and defensive. They will feel abused and insulted and may feel resentful for years. The victim of such an assault may be unwilling to confront the angry person because that person is behaving so irrationally.

Waiting until the angry person is calm and then bringing the matter up for discussion may lead to a clarification of the situation and a new understanding with the individual. If the person is always somewhat angry, that may not be a safe strategy. Never put yourself in a physically unsafe situation just to get an apology.

If you're trying to salvage a relationship with someone whom you care for deeply, and the situation is unsafe, it is best to get professional support.

It would also be wise to question yourself as to why you care for this person more than you care for yourself. Understand that if you are willing to live in a situation where you are physically or emotionally unsafe, you are demonstrating that you do not love or value yourself enough to protect yourself.

It's important to recognize that your feelings are your choice. No one else can make you feel loved, accepted, and positive but you. Support and affirmation from others may make a person feel good, but those feelings are fleeting. Understanding yourself and having positive self-regard sustains an individual even when they are not receiving positive attention from others.

Attitude Dictates Feelings

Your attitude toward your experiences dictates the feelings you are going to have. You make the decisions about the attitudes you will have throughout your life. You can refuse to be offended by what anyone says or does. That is a choice you make many times a day.

As my mother would have said, "When you're offended, consider the source." Sometimes that source will be you. If you take a situation in which you have been offended and look carefully at all the aspects of it, you may find yourself with a different perspective.

Think about asking yourself some of the following questions the next time you're offended by something someone else says or does.

- What did it feel like to you at the time it happened?
- Have you felt that way before?
- What memories has it stirred up?
- Have other similar situations happened to you?
- Is there a pattern of behavior becoming apparent to you?

As you answer these questions to yourself, you may find the situation identifying a hurt within yourself that you've been carrying for a long time.

The offending person may not have known of the hurts you have sustained in the past, or how their words or actions would affect you. They didn't have anything to do with implanting the hurt feeling for the first time. That feeling was already inside you. It was scar tissue from the past that got irritated – scar tissue that needs healing.

It's true that someone in the abusive group could know what they were doing. People in this group have a knack for seeing vulnerabilities in other people. Once we know where our scar tissue is, even abusive people are much less successful in offending us.

The most valuable knowledge we will ever possess is a realistic understanding of our own value and our own failings. Our positive attributes, as well as our weaknesses, are well known to those around us.

Most of the time, our friends enjoy our many positive traits and ignore our faults. Facing our shortcomings with grace helps maintain that humility of spirit that allows us to view our flaws with humor and takes the edge off our rough spots with friends.

"Speak when you're angry
And you'll make the best speech
You'll ever regret."

--Ambrose Bierie

"The last of human freedoms –
The ability to choose one's attitude
In a given set of circumstances."

--Viktor E. Frankl, MD, PhD, *"Man's Search for Meaning"*

5

Protecting Yourself

"No one can make you feel inferior
Without your consent."

--Eleanor Roosevelt

Throughout this book we have talked often of protecting yourself from people who are not committed to living in peace. Learning the following skills takes practice and determination. To help sustain us through trying times, think about the advantages of strengthening one's character to meet difficult situations successfully. This can benefit us in every walk of life.

Personal Agenda

When dealing with people that we do not trust implicitly, we need to have an agenda for ourselves and to know exactly what it is. Set a specific goal for yourself that you can say in a few words and stay tuned in to it.

Especially keep your own goals in mind during interactions with offensive people. Don't allow yourself to be distracted from your goal. That goal can be as simple as leaving a situation within a certain amount of time, or being happy about some aspect of your appearance. It could be as complicated as attaining an advanced degree, or a position in a certain field of endeavor.

Communication Style

Many years ago Robert Alberti and Michael Emmons write a book titled "*Your Perfect Right: Assertiveness & Equality in Your Life and Relationships.*" Now in its 9th Edition, this book details three communication styles that dominate relationships. For the individual who wishes to have more satisfying relationships, studying this book and taking Assertiveness Training will be most rewarding.

Being assertive does not mean being aggressive or controlling of others. Assertive people do not insist that their needs be met no matter how negatively this action impacts others.

Another communication style is the passive approach. These people appear quite gentle in their approach to others, but in reality they have not learned to get their needs met in a straight-forward manner. They depend on other people to notice what they need and be kind enough to offer it to them.

When continually thwarted in their efforts to get their needs met such people often become angry, demanding, and even hysterically insistent that others give them what they want. They may believe that other people are self-centered and don't listen to what they are saying. They don't realize how poorly they are communicating their desires to those around them.

Since they don't understand their own needs, let alone how to get those needs met, passive communicators often partner with the third type, an aggressive communicator. The passive individual seems to think that such a person is strong and knows how to get things done. This, unfortunately, can lead to a lifetime of exploitation and emotional pain, often for both parties.

In truth, an aggressive person often does get what they want from other people, at least for a time. The aggressive approach is to run roughshod over everyone until their own goals are realized. They leave many hurt and angry people in their wake. They take what they want without regard to the needs of others.

If such a person runs into someone more competitive and aggressive than they are, they will do a 180-degree turn and become passive with that particular person. The more aggressive person gets their needs met and the less aggressive person does not.

In contrast with the aggressive person, the assertive person states their desires and position clearly and takes the steps to obtain them if it is reasonable to do so. They don't destroy other people to get to their goals.

The assertive person would be unlikely to get caught in a prolonged battle for control but would endeavor to employ a negotiated approach. If their desire would get them physically assaulted by an angry companion, an assertive person would leave the situation without making an issue of it.

They would then take steps to avoid being put in that position again and would continue to attempt to get their needs met by attempting negotiation with more reasonable people or by investigating other routes to their desired goal.

Which category do you favor as a communication goal?

- Passive people can't say no. They feel guilty when they do.
- Assertive people may say 'yes' or 'no' depending on the situation and whether they are in a position to accommodate a request.
- Aggressive people generally do what they want without regard to the needs of others unless accommodating others will obtain a desired payoff for themselves.

People who communicate assertively are less likely to put themselves into a situation where they offend others or are offended by others. They can live a life that is more peaceful and productive than either the passive or aggressive communication styles.

Hidden Agendas

In protecting yourself, it is important to become as aware of your own hidden agendas and subconscious goals as possible. Desires which we hide from ourselves make us a target since other people are often able to see our vulnerabilities more clearly than we can. Whatever it is in life that you are desirous of having is within your right to have unless it entails deliberately hurting others.

So acknowledge what you want from life. Make a plan and go after that goal. Keep it front and center in your mind. When controlling people try to distract or discourage you, take a deep breath and repeat to yourself that you have a right to your own goals. Then just say "No" to anyone trying to sidetrack you.

Reaction to Abusive Situations

If you do become involved in an abusive situation with someone, forgive yourself and forgive them right away. Don't blame either yourself or them. You both have the right to be who you are and to do and say what you choose to do and say.

Going over and over the situation leads your subconscious to think that the situation has occurred again and again. You will stir up the painful feelings each time you rehearse the event in your mind. You are taking another beating as far as your inner self is concerned. This is very hard on an individual's self-esteem and peace of mind.

The faster you can forgive, the easier it is on you. If you keep rehearsing the scenario in your mind, it will get worse with the repetition and you will suffer even more.

Controlling Others

When we stop attempting to control other people, the habit of forgiveness comes easily. *The more we try to control other people, the more offended we will be.*

One can't forgive while thinking "They shouldn't have done that to me." It is necessary to allow the other person their own behavior and the responsibility for that behavior. If we try to control their behavior toward us and they don't care to do as we want, or change their behavior to what we believe is appropriate, we stay resentful and feeling lonely and abused.

Letting Go

Peace comes when we let go of abusive people, at least emotionally. We may find ourselves in daily contact with such folks because of our jobs or a family situation. We can be civil, even gracious, and still stay personally uninvolved. We need to let them be who they are and let them deal with their own behavioral consequences.

Taking Charge of Our Own Life

Remaining in a situation with a person who treats us with disrespect means that we are refusing, for whatever reason, to take the responsibility for our own happiness. There may be circumstances where we have to compromise our happiness for a time but those situations need to be worked on daily with as many tools as we can learn.

We need to take charge of our own life and choose to live in uplifting surroundings with people who treat us well. This may mean learning to take risks with our comfort levels. It's normal to be uncomfortable in situations where we haven't been before. Even negative situations become comfortable with familiarity. If we avoid challenging ourselves with new experiences and new people, we may not live the life we have a right to enjoy.

Taking Charge of Our Own Feelings

This is true also with feelings. Keep in mind that your previous experiences have taught you how to identify the feelings you are having. Question whether or not the name you put on the feeling you're having in a situation might be identified differently by someone else.

Even good feelings can being discomfort and anxiety to someone who has had limited experience with good things happening in their lives. Try new situations, new kinds of people, and keep it up until new experiences and meeting new people are wonderfully exciting to you.

Healthy Body, Healthy Mind

It is difficult to maintain a healthy mind and spirit in a neglected physical body. Take the time necessary to keep your body toned, properly fed, and rested.

Most people need seven or eight hours of sleep every night. Twenty minutes in the afternoon for meditation or some rest can leave a person feeling refreshed, mentally sharp, and better able to cope with the stresses of the day.

It isn't just athletes that need exercise. Everyone needs daily conditioning appropriate for what they are physically able to do. People with sedentary jobs are especially vulnerable to evening fatigue and the desire to be a couch potato. Drink a glass of water and take a leisurely walk for a few minutes to stimulate the desire to exercise.

Keep in mind that law of physics: A body in motion tends to stay in motion, a body at rest tends to stay at rest. Push for that burst of energy to change the pattern you are in. The human body was constructed for movement. Lack of movement presages decay.

Food intake is very personal but everyone knows the foods that agree with them and those that don't. Think of your body as a finely-tuned car. You wouldn't put saltwater or mayonnaise in your car and expect it to run. Don't do something similar to your body. It was created to run on veggies, fruit, and protein. To demand that it function well on sugary treats and potato chips is insane. Take the time to eat properly.

"Progress is impossible without change, and
Those who cannot change their minds,
Cannot change anything."

--George Bernard Shaw

6

Forgiving Ourselves

"Few suffer more than those
Who refuse to forgive themselves."

--Mike Norton, *Fighting for Redemption*

The organs of our physical bodies are very busy places with work to do every second of our lives. The last thing we want is for an organ to shut down or take a siesta. For the organs of our bodies to slow down means illness and without intervention, perhaps death.

Our brains are no exception. There are neurons firing; blood flowing through the vessels; chemicals making their way to receptor sites; a flurry of constant action which keeps our brain cells alive and functioning. The more we stimulate our brain, the more efficient it becomes.

Even asleep our brains continue to work and when we wake sometimes we remember flashes of dreams we've had. Our dreams rarely make sense to us, flowing from scene to scene without the restrictions of time, gravity, or any other physical reality.

Awake, we perceive the brain's activity through our many senses of sight, sound, touch, and thoughts. Sometimes our thoughts are well ordered and serve to help us understand our environment or find successful ways to communicate with other people. Sometimes our thoughts are a surprise to us, with ideas popping in unbidden, with memories surfacing and feelings stirred up that we would just as soon leave forgotten.

At times we may be astounded at a memory which flashes through our mind and we wonder why that particular memory surfaced at that particular time. We may think, "Wow! I'd forgotten all about that event! It happened so many years ago. I wonder what made me think of it right now."

It serves us well to keep in mind that every experience, every feeling, every sight, every smell, we've ever had is recorded in our brain for all time. Unless we suffer from a brain-wasting disease where structures of our brain actually disintegrate, every memory can be tapped by the stimulation of the brain where that memory is stored.

It serves us well to protect the images and experiences we place in our brains because they will be with us forever. Through the random firing of neurons throughout our lives, we may find ourselves viewing these past events, movie scenes, or feelings at times we'd rather not be reminded of them.

This happens with situations where forgiveness is involved as well as other more peaceful experiences. It's disconcerting when an event that we were sure we had worked through, and we're been sure that we had forgiven all the participating parties, suddenly surfaces with all the energy it had when it first occurred.

At such times many folks begin to ruminate about the incident again, and question their feelings, and doubt the sincerity of their forgiveness. For many people, this begins another painful examination of the event, the hurt feelings they had, and their efforts to find closure and peace.

When this happens, the first thing to consider is whether or not you really did forgive the other person. Ask yourself: "Do I wish to hurt this person who offended me?"

If you can say, "No, I don't wish to hurt this person for what they did to me," know without a doubt that you have forgiven this person. You have passed the acid test of forgiveness. You have released them to their own behavior and responsibility.

The situation is in your memory bank and you may think of it from time to time but it is no longer an event that you need to ponder. Distract yourself and the energy will be gone from the memory.

Don't allow yourself to ruminate on this memory if it resurfaces. It's done and over. Don't waste your time with it. As you live your life and more experiences are sorted and stored by your brain, it will be less likely that your randomly firing neurons will find this particular memory again.

If you spend time brooding over the incident and trying to determine if you really did forgive or if you still have residual anger and humiliation, you are giving the memory energy. Your brain will think the event is happening again, and will store it as a new memory and you will be more likely to think of it again.

Every time you think of the situation and give it energy, it will be as if you have gone through the same experience again. This can be exhausting to your psyche and lead an individual into a pattern of angry thoughts and a lack of trust in relationships.

Some people may be thinking, "But this memory is so strong. How can I distract myself from it?"

It's worth noting that we do have control of our thoughts. We can think the thoughts we want to think. *Our thoughts do not have control of us, we have control of our thoughts.* If people were to act out or say all the random thoughts that cross their minds, this would be a wild world! We can choose the thoughts we want to think, and ponder the thoughts we want to think about more deeply. We do not have to allow any thought that enters our mind to take root and influence our mood or behavior.

To distract yourself, do whatever you can do: pet the dog, call a friend, bake a cake, read a book, take a shower, touch your toes a couple of times, or simply tell yourself: "I wonder where that thought came from. I'd rather think about the flowers I plan to plant in the garden next spring." And then start planning your garden.

If you want a foolproof method of distracting yourself quickly from any thought, start counting backwards from 100 (or 1000). It's especially difficult to count backwards by an odd number such as seven, three, or nine. Five is too easy for most folks, but it will still work. The part of your mind that does math is in a totally different area than memories and you cannot think of both math and memories at the same time.

Just remember, your mind will go along with whatever you tell it to think about. You are not at the mercy of your mind's efforts to exercise itself.

While some people will question if they have been forgiving when such memories surface, other people will blame themselves that the event happened.

They feel they should have been smart enough to have had a snappy answer for their abuser that would have put the other person in their place, or they should have been smart enough to have avoided the situation, or it was their neediness that allowed the situation to become what it became.

These people find themselves taking the blame for the situation because of their perceived personal failures whatever they imagine them to be. They do not see themselves as the perfect and/or powerful person they need to believe they are.

To find peace, these people must forgive themselves for their part in the unpleasant experience they keep remembering.

What makes it so hard to forgive ourselves? If forgiving implies change, to forgive ourselves is to admit that we are not as perfect as we try to be, as we want to be, as we tried to be as little children to gain our parents love.

Some of us will see the need to change as a failure so large that others have not only noticed our behavior but have been injured by it. If we do not have a realistic view of ourselves, admitting an imperfection in our character or abilities can be a confrontation we just don't want to have. Additionally, there may be an area in our character where we simply cannot admit there could be a flaw.

If we don't allow ourselves to examine all of the areas of our personality with the knowledge that some aspects of ourselves may need some fine-tuning, we may suffer our entire lives. No one is perfect. No one has all the answers. To acknowledge our short-comings and try to improve is a mark of personal and emotional strength.

Perhaps, as an exercise in forgiving ourselves, we need to bring an event to mind over which we are anguishing and try to look at this experience with as little defensiveness as we can muster.

If this is the first time you've tried this, start with an event that is troubling to you but not earthshaking. It's better to take little steps into self-knowledge, than to try to take giant leaps, find the path too steep, and stop the climb.

Inner knowledge comes slowly, so give your mind time to absorb what you are discovering about yourself. Some of our discoveries will be unpleasant to face. Some of our discoveries will be challenging. Some discoveries will be pleasantly surprising.

Always be gentle with yourself, but don't hide from yourself as you ask yourself the following questions. It's best to write down your answers since some thoughts may be fleeting and you may want to remember them later.

So relax, take a deep breath, and assure yourself that you are a good person who wants to become all that you can become. The questions listed here are only a guide since every situation is different. You may think of other questions that are very pertinent to your personal circumstances. If, on reflection, a question does not apply to you, skip it.

When you are ready to explore the event you have decided upon, start asking yourself these question:

- Have you found yourself in this kind of situation frequently?
- What was your demeanor?
- Were you enjoying yourself?
- Were you enjoying the discomfort of someone else?
- Were you frightened?
- Were you being controlling of others?
- Was someone trying to control you?
- Were you anxious or upset?
- Do you understand the situation differently now compared to when it was happening?
- Was your behavior, or were your statements, considered unreasonable by others, perhaps even by yourself?
- Did you feel fearful of other people involved?
- Are you often fearful of people or new situations?
- How could you have handled the situation differently?

- Does it make sense for you to feel guilty over the situation?
- Did you handle the situation as capably as the skills you had *at that time* allowed?
- Are you starting to see patterns in your behavior?
- Is there a humorous aspect to the situation which you have not been able to appreciate?

Think carefully about your observations as you look at the event from a different perspective.

- Have you talked the situation over with those involved?
- Have you made the necessary changes in yourself to avoid a similar situation from occurring?
- If you have made changes, why are you still upset with yourself?
- Has another person involved in the situation refused to talk with you?
- Were you willing to discuss the event with them in a conciliatory manner?
- If you were willing to make the effort to pursue a mutual understanding of the situation, why does this remain a problem for you?
- Do you miss the person and the activities you used to enjoy with them?
- Have you made efforts to build new friendships?
- If this were a friend trying to make peace with themselves over this situation, how would you advise them?

- Would you think it made sense for your friend to continue to criticize themselves over this situation?

Perhaps it's time to acknowledge your own positive intentions and let this situation rest. No one is perfect. Take the steps necessary to avoid a repetition of this behavior. Isn't that all you would ask of someone else?

An even different perspective revolves around the emotional reactions we undergo after an unfortunate experience that results in feelings of resentment toward another or oneself.

- What feeling emerges as you brood over the situation?
- Is this a negative or a positive feeling?
- Do you enjoy this feeling even slightly?
- How is this feeling beneficial to you?
- Does this feeling point out to you your worthiness or unworthiness as a human being?
- Do you give yourself permission to avoid challenging activities by telling yourself that you are not as valuable or as skilled as other people?
- Where did you first get the idea that you were of little value?
- Do you recognize that you are as valuable as every other person on this earth?

Some folks do not want forgiveness for their past actions as it would eliminate an impediment to living as fully as other people. If this sounds like what you are doing, it may be time for an emotional housecleaning with the aid of a competent psychotherapist. You only get one life. Don't live it in a closet of fear or pride.

Anxiety Reactions

While examining your motives for not forgiving yourself, catalog how you feel physically when you think of unforgettable situations where you believe you behaved poorly.

- Does your body begin to sweat?
- Do you get a headache?
- Do your muscles become tense or rigid?
- Do you start to shake, or make involuntary movements?
- Is it hard to breathe?
- Are you able to talk and express what you are feeling?
- Is your speech coherent?
- Do you ramble without a clear focus?
- Do these memories sometimes wake you from sleep?
- Do such memories seem to attack you just as you're falling asleep, waking you back up with a spasm of anxiety?
- Are there moments or hours of your recent life where you cannot remember what you were doing?
- Do you regularly look out for the wishes of others at the expense of your own needs and desires?

If some of these physical reactions are present for you, it is possible that you are not dealing with the memories of a situation where you can't forgive yourself. Perhaps the situation was so traumatic for you that you have a disabling anxiety condition such as Post Traumatic Stress Disorder.

There is a difference between anxiety over situations where you are not forgiving yourself for unwise, insensitive, or bullying behavior, and the anxiety that comes from traumatic situations in which you have been involved.

If your core self is sufficiently shocked by any kind of ordeal, the resulting trauma may be disabling for life without appropriate attention.

For instance, you may have caused an accident where someone was injured. Perhaps you were an injured victim, and you are berating yourself for not responding effectively enough to protect yourself or others from physical injury or a bullying episode.

Predictable, methodical abuse over a period of time can leave a person with a pervasive sense of helplessness. Rape can leave the individual, male or female, with a sense of defilement and rage as well as helplessness. They may find they vacillate between these extremes of emotion and behavior which leaves them feeling confused and weary.

All of these syndromes are treatable by a psychotherapist experienced with the specific condition. It is important for the individual to be in a situation where the community surrounding them models understanding and support of their healing. If the individual is not in such a community, efforts need to be made to change their environment to a more healing atmosphere. Community is critical in the healing of anxiety.

Understand there is a difference between various types of memories and the anxiety accompanying them. Proceed with wisdom to find your solution.

"Letting ourselves be forgiven

Is one of the most difficult healings we will undertake,

And one of the most fruitful."

--Stephen Levine, *A Year to live:*
How to Live This Year as if it Were Your Last

7

Looking Back

"This is certain, that a man that studieth revenge

Keeps his wounds green,

Which otherwise would heal and do well."

--Francis Bacon

Feelings are not facts. That statement is hard to believe because emotions feel so real. Strictly speaking, however, feelings are actually the result of a sudden burst of chemicals within our bodies in response to an occurrence in our environment.

It's how we interpret that newly felt energy that gives it a name. We interpret that energy based on our perceptions of what's happening around us. One person may feel a burst of energy and call it excitement while another person in the same situation will call that burst of energy fear.

As an example, let's say that Bob and Carl are walking home one sunny afternoon when they see in the distance a large, black dog dangling a strong but broken chain. Both feel a sudden surge of energy as they realize the dog is trotting right toward them.

"I do believe that's my neighbor's big Labrador Retriever, Bosco," Bob says to himself as he gets closer to the dog. "They were having some construction work done today and were going to chain Bosco so he wouldn't get in the way. It looks like he broke his chain and went for a stroll. I'd better take him home so he won't get lost."

Bob calls Bosco to him, pats him on the shoulder as he gathers up the end of the chain and together they walk home. How is Bob feeling? He's pleased with himself for doing his neighbor a good turn. He's enjoying the company of Bosco whom he has known since he was a puppy. It's a pleasant interlude in his day.

But for Carl, the story is quite different. He looks at the large, black dog with a strong but broken chain and feels the urge to run in the opposite direction. His palms begin to sweat and his heart starts racing. All he can think of is the time when, as a child, he was badly bitten by a dog. The strong, broken chain only makes the dog look more threatening.

"If the dog's owners thought he needed a chain that strong, they know this dog could be vicious," he tells himself. "This dog was strong enough to break that chain. I'm in deep trouble."

Two different people with two different experiences with dogs in the past and they are reacting with very different feelings about the dog in present time.

Bob would undoubtedly laugh if someone would tell him he should be feeling fearful of his neighbor's dog. At the same time, Carl's discomfort would be exacerbated if someone were to tell him that being afraid of this lumbering, friendly dog was irrational.

This is the power of the past in our daily life. We live in the present but every day is colored by the experiences we have gone through in prior days. Whether the past that haunts us is a miserable childhood or a marriage that ends in a devastating divorce, the events we have lived through are buried in our psyches and affect our current experiences.

It is important for each of us to understand a fact of human nature. In every experience, in every decision that affects our lives, human beings weigh their different options and the probable consequences. They choose the behavior that makes the most sense based on their knowledge, experience, and the options they are aware are open to them at that time.

This is true whether it is a parent ill-prepared to raise children for whatever reason, or a spouse who cheats, lies or succumbs to an addiction that eventually destroys the marriage.

No one deliberately chooses the path that they know will make their situation worse. To an onlooker, they may have done just that. But to the individual making the choice, it was the best decision they could make at the time. The fact that other people have been severely hurt by their behavior may upset them, but everyone can always defend the path they have chosen.

For the people who must pay a terrible price for the poor choices of their parents, spouses, or friends, the reasoning for their choice is not a consolation. As soon as they are able, it is important for the injured party to recognize the poor choices that have affected them, make a decision with their free will to forgive the person who has harmed them, and form a resolution that the behavior they have been subjected to will not be repeated by them.

When people have been subjected to brutal behavior there is often a strong inclination to perform the same behavior on someone else. Perhaps this is a form of "retaliation in absentia" against the original perpetrator.

It may be that the individual is unsure if they should be unhappy that they were treated in a hurtful way by the very people that were supposed to love them. They may feel a need to behave toward someone else as they were treated in an effort to see if other people are as upset by their action as they were when the behavior was done to them.

Whatever the reason, an injured person needs to stand firm with their conviction that the behavior was wrong when it was done to them and the behavior is going to stop with them. They are not going to pass such treatment on to another spouse, or a new generation of children, or even a casual acquaintance.

They must stand against the injurious behavior and say with conviction and determination, "It stops with me. I was injured by that behavior and I will not pass it on."

With that conscious statement comes a cleansing, and in the future when they find themselves in the position of consciously choosing not to pass that behavior on, they will find that a healing of the resentment is taking place. Taking such a position is not easy without support. Individuals who are in this position may well find it advantageous to join a support group with similar stories, or to obtain private counselling to help come to terms with their histories.

Keep in mind that when people are interacting with someone who has injured them in the past, they need to remember the behavior and refuse to allow it to be repeated in the present.

No one has to continue in a coercive relationship. They may need to express very directly to the aggressive party that they do not wish to be talked to, or treated, in a demeaning manner again. They also need to make it clear that the behavior is unacceptable and if it continues, they will leave the relationship.

If this confrontation will cause them too much fear, they need to avoid the offending person. When they are emotionally and mentally able to define the boundaries of their relationship, they may be able to attempt a reconciliation.

Sometimes children haven't understood the stresses their parents were in and such a conversation is very healing. There are situations where a parent may have been so overwrought by life's pressures that they slid into a psychotic state for a time, deeply injuring their children in the process. When they regain a more injuring their children in the process. When they regain a more rational mental state, their understanding of their previous behavior may be minimal. If their behavior has become more acceptable, it could be time to re-establish the relationship.

Parents need to know that no parent does everything perfectly for every child every day. Unfortunate occurrences do happen and children see situations very differently from the adults around them.

When children, at any age, do confront a parent with grievances, it's best for the parent to simply say, "I'm sorry that happened. Let's talk about it." The parent then needs to do a lot of listening and re-assure the child of their love.

This is difficult for some parents to do. They felt justified in doing what they did in the situation and see this as a loss of their authority. Children of any age rarely see it this way.

Children love their parents and want to know their parents love them. As a general rule, they are very forgiving of their parents, but sometimes their childhood was very confusing to them. They do need to understand why their parents treated them the way they did. An apology by a parent goes a very long way in levelling out a child's hurt feelings and re-establishing a positive relationship.

Sometimes children have questions about situations that occurred in the family that they didn't understand. Children may blame themselves for problems that had nothing to do with them. A parent's explanation may serve to ease a long standing feeling of guilt.

Sibling rivalries that start in childhood and extend into adulthood are all too common. Keep in mind that behaviors in childhood are not necessarily the behaviors carried into adult years. People live and learn. If you're in a discordant relationship with a sibling, try talking it out before giving up the relationship or keeping the sibling at arm's length. It may be that you've both changed over the years and a positive, healthy relationship is possible.

In some situations, a declaration of "we change our relationship or I'm gone" could be met with physical and emotional force. It is important to recognize that when another person is unstable and dependent upon the relationship, they could be willing to protect the security of the relationship with violence. In such instances it is imperative that the victim gain the assistance of friends and authorities to escape the situation.

At times, an acquaintance may not accept that they have done anything wrong and are deeply offended at being confronted. If the abusive behavior continues, the victim will need to protect them-selves in whatever manner is necessary for their continued good health. This may include never being alone with the other person or removing themselves from the relationship permanently.

If this is necessary, such a parting can be done without regrets. Both parties have the right to be who they are and be safe -- mentally, emotionally, and physically.

"Forgiveness means it finally becomes unimportant
That you hit back."

--Ann Lamott

"We begin to forgive by choosing to forgive...

By deciding, not by feeling.

Our feelings don't lead us to forgive.

Most times, our feelings lead us the other way.

That's why a person has to decide to forgive first.

Our feelings always follow along behind our decisions."

--Andy Andrews, *The Heart Mends: A Story of Second Chances*

8

Bringing Change into Our Lives

"Yesterday, I was clever so I wanted to change the world.

Today, I am wise, so I am changing myself."

--Rumi

At some point in everyone's life, there is a time when we realize that to obtain from life what we really desire, we are going to have to make some changes in our behaviors and our attitudes. The next big question that must be answered is: What do we change and how do we change it.

Before we can make a decision about these questions, we may need to sort out how we feel about changing behaviors that we have learned in our family home or among our earliest friends.

Our behaviors are very important to us. Our families taught us behaviors and attitudes that had been taught to them by their families and that were compatible with the knowledge and experiences that they had encountered. Additionally, both parents had already changed some of their behaviors and attitudes as necessary to accommodate their partner's needs and beliefs in order to form their own family traditions. Together they are passing on the treasured wisdom of many generations to their children.

As children move into the worlds of school, friends, and work, they have already changed some of the ways their parents had taught them. If you don't believe me, ask your parents. One of the commonest statements I hear from parents with adult children is the plaintive comment: "I don't know what happened to him (or her). He was always such a happy kid. Now he's just plain ornery." Or, "She (or he) was the sweetest child you can possibly imagine. Now she's gotten so tough acting."

Understand that change is not a condemnation of past behavior. It is a reality of living. As long as a person is alive, they can, and will, make changes to their behavior and attitudes. Such change is usually unconscious and in response to external pressures from the environment.

Change and recognizing the need for it can be thought of as personal growth. However, before we can embark on deliberately changing a behavior, we need to take the time to carefully ponder whether or not we really want to change.

Different behaviors have different rewards. What were the rewards for our old behaviors? Were there hidden rewards that we could count on with the old behaviors? How will those rewards change with our new behaviors or attitudes?

Do we know for sure what the new behavior is that we are wanting to learn? Or are we aware that we are not relating as well as we want to with other people but we're not sure what we should be trying to change about ourselves?

If someone really doesn't know what they want to change, they need to spend some time studying the behavior of other people who do seem to be relating to people in the way that they wish they could. Look for common denominators in the behaviors of these people.

Do they smile a lot? Do they tell jokes? Do they seem to know someone everywhere they go? Are they helpful to others or do they wait to be asked for help? Do they seem to have a lot of energy? Do they have pets at home? How do these people differ from each other? What do you admire in their personality?

It's a good idea to try on some of the more obvious behaviors for a few days and see how they feel. Some behaviors may feel comfortable from the first time they are tried. For a shy person to try smiling broadly, shaking hands with strangers, and telling quick little jokes for a laugh might give them the most uncomfortable afternoon of their life. They might also find it was lots of fun.

In my workshops, I have people learn how to shake hands while looking the other person directly in the eyes. We go over and over this exercise. Within minutes, the room is rocking with gales of laughter and excited talking. Nearly everyone is clearly embarrassed.

Many people do not know how to shake hands as if they wanted to touch the other person. Giving a warm handshake with the palms touching can be very difficult. Looking the other person in the eyes at the same time can be quite unnerving to someone who is not accustomed to eye contact.

And then I ask them to do a third action. Instantly, as they look at the other person, I want them to see something to like about that person. It could be the color of their eyes, or the way they wear their hair. It could be the style of clothing they've chosen, or the warmth of their smile.

Their homework for the week is to become very adept at liking something about everyone they pass on the street or with whom they otherwise come in contact. They are not to say a word, just look at these strangers and like something about them as they pass them.

The result of this activity is that they become friendlier people, because they are suddenly in a friendlier world. People respond to being liked, even silently.

Another result is that my students find themselves less fearful of other people. It's difficult to be afraid of a person when you have noticed something you like about them, and see that they are smiling a little shyly at you.

A good routine for change is to determine whom among your acquaintances, at home or at work, have behaviors that you admire and wish you were more like. Pick one or two of these people and determine which single behavior each of them has that you most want to learn.

Try to imitate this behavior as closely as possible until it becomes your own. With this person frequently in your life you are able to see them demonstrate this action many times in many different situations. Keep trying to make this behavior your own until you find that you automatically react to people the way you wanted to when you first chose this behavior.

Then look for another behavior in someone else that you would like to incorporate into your behavior patterns.

Children do this automatically. We've all heard of the three-year-old that will suddenly, usually in front of company, burst forth with some rather salty language. Both parents often cry out in unison, "He didn't get that from me!"

Keep in mind that we can choose how we change, if we change, and when we change. We have the right to decide what kind of person we will be.

Another source for ideas on how to change into a more likeable person can be found in the Dale Carnegie book, *"How to Win Friends and Influence People."* This book details behaviors that are acknowledged internationally as basic to being a charming and friendly person.

But suppose the change a person needs to make is more critical than becoming a person that other people enjoy knowing.

Suppose it's some form of addiction that is destroying their relationships such as drinking heavily, eating poorly, recreational drug use, sexual infidelities and the like.

To start they need to think carefully about the rewards they are receiving from the behavior they need to change. They need to think about   the obvious rewards as well as the hidden rewards. It's also necessary to question the obvious rewards as well as the hidden rewards in the new behavior they desire to adopt.

The obvious rewards are usually very clear – looking healthier, making more money, having a better job, keeping your spouse, the list of obvious rewards seems endless.

Figuring out the hidden rewards can be very challenging. When we hide a fact about ourselves from ourselves we are trying to avoid recognizing something we know we will find painful. The information is there but so is the wound.

For example, if we changed our behavior, we could have a better job. That's obvious. What isn't obvious is that with the better job will come more responsibilities, and we're cracking under the stress of the responsibilities we already have.

For example, if we changed our behavior, we'd keep our spouse but we'd have to listen to their endless nagging about our other deficiencies. Maybe the truth is that we want to leave the marriage, but we don't want to be alone and we can't believe that anyone else would want to marry us.

Searching ourselves for subconscious blocks to changing behaviors is critical. There may be an aversion to change which is based in subconscious fears or beliefs that are difficult to pinpoint or accept. It's often necessary to get professional help to uncover such barriers to change. A support group of people who have successfully managed to overcome self-defeating behaviors is often a positive resource.

However, it is also possible that behaviors based on self-defeating impulsive reactions may have a neurological substrate that has little to do with long term rewards.

Looking at changing difficult behaviors from a cognitive perspective has been gaining acceptance in scientific circles lately. In response to preferred temptations, some people behave impulsively which makes change problematic. Thoughts that could help them resist such temptations are much slower to surface and are weak compared to the strength of the impulsive response.

Cognitive training which requires the brain to stretch its memory ability and to think quickly and flexibly appears to be part of the solution.* This type of training has to be varied in content and design and to have no upper limits so that the individual is able to continue to stretch their mental capacity. Coupled with response inhibition training techniques, this study shows promise in helping impulsive people gain control over temptations.

Another point to remember in attempting change for addictions that relate to physical functioning is that metabolic dependencies may have developed, as well as behavioral habits. It's wise to have a thorough medical screening if efforts to change an addiction to sugar, food, alcohol, or drugs persists in a return to the addiction. Your body may need medical support in order for your efforts to be successful.

*Houben, K., Wiers, R>W>, and Jansen, A. (2011) University of Amsterdam, *Getting a Grip on Drinking Behavior: Training Working Memory to Reduce Alcohol Abuse*, Psychological Science Abstract: www. ncbi.nem.nih.gov/pubmed/21685380

"When we are no longer able to change a situation,
We are challenged to change ourselves."

--Viktor E. Frankl, MD, PhD, *"Man's Search for Meaning"*

TEN STEPS TO PERMANENT CHANGE

1. Feeling dissatisfaction with your current situation and the rewards obtained by your behaviors

2. Gaining insight into your current behaviors and the rewards possible with new behaviors.

3. Motivation to change must be stronger than the desire to remain in your present state.

4. Study your current behaviors and how to incorporate new behaviors as a habit.

5. Recognize current behaviors as a familiar, comfortable habit that you have acquired through your lifestyle, your family culture, or your friends.

6. Confront any perceptions that changing your habit will imply that you've been wrong or weak in the past.

7. Obtain permission to change the old behaviors from yourself or from someone else if you can't give it to yourself. Your behaviors are a choice you make. You can behave any way that you decide is best for you. That is your right.

8. Practice your new habit.

9. Acknowledge that change can be slow and there will be slips. Give yourself time to recognize and tweak the weak spots in your new routine.

10. Follow-through. Maintain the change daily for three-and-a-half weeks to accomplish a life-time habit.

"Nothing enables us to forgive

Like knowing in our hearts

That we have been forgiven."

--Lewis B. Smedes

9

How to Have a Healing Conversation

"It takes one person to forgive,
It takes two people to be reunited."

--Lewis B. Smedes

Talking to someone who has offended you is not easy. Talking about how they offended you is even harder. It's even more painful to hear them say that you have offended them. That's a toughie, right? But it is part of a healing conversation.

It's very important for both of you to know that *under-standing what another person says is <u>not the same</u> as agreeing with them.* Make your differences clear. With enough understanding of each other's positions, priorities will begin to emerge with which both of you can live comfortably.

Many people go through life without ever confronting anybody when their feelings are hurt. They live with unresolved conflict in their hearts day in and day out, year in and year out.

What they are actually doing is avoiding their own responsibility to themselves. Saying: "We have to talk about what just happened. That really hurt my feelings." would entail confronting their own feelings as well as their friend's behavior.

Many people would rather just go along, living through perceived abusive situations rather than run the risk of losing friends. They may also be fearful of not being able to express themselves well enough to communicate their needs successfully.

This inability to communicate one's needs and feelings can be devastating in a marriage. Some people won't run the risk of telling their mate their needs until they've become so hurt that they just don't care anymore.

When they do share, however subtly, that they've had enough of their partner's habits, they will require their mate to make instant changes. Their mate, being confused, shocked, probably offended, may not be able to make instant behavioral adjustments or even understand this sudden need for contrition.

Their mate is justified in considerable anger if the non-communicative party's reaction is to leave the relationship saying, "See, they don't care enough about my feelings to even try to change." They will not understand why their spouse withheld their real feelings for so many years. They will feel betrayed and abandoned.

So let's discuss some basic parameters that will make it easier on both parties to share their feelings. As you work to have a healing conversation with your partner keep in mind what a special time this is for your relationship. You are both at a point *at the very same time* when you are open to changing the dynamics of your bond with each other to a deeper place of trust and caring.

FOCUS

Make your #1 aim a deeper understanding of your partner or your friend. Work toward a clear explanation of what was perceived and how it made both of you feel. Deciding between the two of you how to avoid such a problem in the future should be your objective. *Winning, getting your way, or defending yourself, is not the purpose of this conversation.* Change, perhaps for both of you, is the goal.

TOPIC

The first step is to avoid surprise. Bombshells are not a smart way to begin a conversation that is meant to bring healing to your relationship. Tell your spouse, partner, or friend the topic you wish to discuss with them so that they have time to collect their thoughts on the matter.

PRIVACY

There should be privacy from other adults. Do not answer the telephone, pager, text, or doorbell. No one is more important than your partner and this commitment to communicate.

TIME

Agree to a time frame that is good for both of you. Neither of you should be tired or have pressing demands on your mind. Agree on a time to stop the discussion before you start.

If you have to stop the discussion before an agreement is reached, arrange another time to continue the matter. It is essential that you both honor this commitment to resume your talk.

If one party finds themselves overwhelmed by the discussion, take the time to stop for a rest. If necessary agree to table the topic and agree to another time to continue the discussion. It is essential that you both honor this appointment to resume your talk.

LOCATION

Pick a neutral location to meet. The bedroom or bathroom is not a neutral location. Choose a room such as a living room, family room, or kitchen. Taking a walk together is often a good way to have such a talk for people who might be uncomfortable looking directly at each other. It is also an excellent way to dissipate physical energies that might otherwise inhibit the conversation.

CHILDREN

There should be no children awake or present since they will want the attention of one or both of you at various times. Children could also be upset or misunderstand what they hear.

SECRECY

Sometimes it is necessary to protect a marriage or a friendship by keeping friends, relatives, and other people and their pet peeves and biases out of your relationship. Never reveal the content of your meeting to others. They won't forget what you have said. Some people who love you may not love your spouse or friend and may use what you have told them to put a wedge into your relationship.

If you must share what is occurring between yourself and your partner, find a professional counselor who is bound by confidentiality.

DRESS

Both parties need to be fully clothed for this meeting. Nudity, even partial nudity, plays on the emotions and may cause an individual to be agreeable and/or submissive when it is not in their best interest or in the interest of good communication.

FOOD AND DRINK

Talking after a meal can be a relaxing, positive approach to discussion. Sharing a cup of coffee or tea in one's living room or kitchen also helps bring about a relaxing atmosphere.

Do not drink alcohol at such a meeting. You need to be able to think very clearly and alcohol will inhibit that ability. If you or your partner feels a difficult discussion without an alcoholic drink is impossible, there is an alcohol dependence that needs to be dealt with medically before any honest discussion can take place.

VOICE

Consciously lower your voice as you talk. Do not allow it to climb to a higher register. Do not interrupt each other. Do not allow your voice tone to attack the other person. Do not use sarcasm, teasing, or attempts at humor. Do not bring any form of verbal weapons into this meeting. All of these tactics can be misunderstood and can make the situation volatile.

THE DISCUSSION

- Share your thoughts in a calm, agreeable manner.
- Attack the problem, not the other person or their motives.
- Do not belittle each other's position, perceptions or feelings.
- State your position, your feelings, and your memories regarding the topic
- Listen carefully to their responses.
- Be sure each of you has ample time to explain your thoughts and feelings.
- Do not interrupt the other person as they are talking.
- Do not defend yourself against the other's person's feelings and perceptions of what occurred. They are entitled to their feelings and they are sharing something deeply personal with you. Listen. Let them know you have heard and understand how they have perceived the incident.

- Take turns talking. People tend to stop listening after two minutes. They may lose track of what's being said. Their own feelings may interfere with their listening ability. So take the problem in easy steps, stop talking and let your partner state their position.

- Stay in present time and on the present topic. Do not bring up other problems or past grievances that may exist between the two of you. Such examples distract from the current topic and will make the discussion confusing.

- Avoid commenting on what the other person has said. State *your* position, *your* feelings and *your* memories regarding the topic.

- If you don't understand something, ask a question in a way to help the other person clarify their position. *A major temptation when a person is feeling hurt and misunderstood is to ask a question designed to force the other person to be more aware of, or sensitive to, their position.* **This form of question will destroy the trust between you and end the session.**

- If your partner asks you a question that turns the conversation to their needs simply state: "That question doesn't help me tell you about my thoughts and feelings in this matter. We should probably save that question until it's your turn."

- Both parties need to know that they will have the chance to express their feelings in this non-threatening discussion.

- If you feel that the other person keeps saying the same thing over and over, *you need to understand that they do not believe that you have heard them.* You need to reflect back to them what you have heard them say and ask if that is what they meant. If it is, the person should be able to move to the next level of discussion. If it isn't what they were attempting to make you understand, the person can try again to clarify their position using different words. Understanding what each person is trying to say is critical to a healing discussion.

- Sometimes the way a topic is brought up may be offensive to one or the other party in such a discussion. If you can get past the initial presentation, you may find that both of you have similar concerns regarding your relationship.

It is an unfortunate truth that there are people who are unable to participate in a healing conversation or to listen to another person without judgment. They are unable to put their own emotions aside long enough to listen to the needs of another person.

If you have tried to talk to such a person and felt thwarted in your efforts to resolve conflicts, and still want to work on the relationship, it's time to call on professional help.

"I can always forgive where I understand."

--Jude Morgan, *Indiscretion*

10

The Physical Effects of Anger and Resentment on the Body

"Holding onto Anger is like grasping a hot coal
With the intent of throwing it at someone else;
You are the one who gets burned."

--Sidharthma Gautama Buddha

Think back to a time when you were suddenly aware that you were being disrespected, undervalued, or otherwise treated in a negative manner. Can you remember how it felt to be in your body at that moment?

For just a second, it seems like time stops, and then you can feel that flush of anger surging through your veins, your muscles tense, and your heart beats faster as you instinctively prepare to defend yourself. Your body has gone into a survival posture.

Your adrenal glands have begun to pump the stress hormone cortisol into your system for a quick burst of energy and strength. Your blood pressure and heart rate increase and chemicals pour into your blood stream to prepare to clot your blood so that you won't be as likely to bleed to death in case of injury.

It's a system in place for all mammals. It's called the fight or flight reaction and it serves us well in times of emergency.

However, when we live in a state of constant anger and resentment because of unresolved issues, this life-saving reaction can take a deadly toll on our physical bodies. When these chemicals are released into our bodies over a prolonged period of time, we create an environment favorable for many diseases.

A blood sugar imbalance can occur due to hormone imbalances which impact the balance of glucose. Cortisol, human growth hormone, glucagon and epinephrine can all lead to higher levels of glucose in the blood stream in times of stress. This is the most common cause of high blood sugars in times of illness or surgery. Occasionally, an overabundance of insulin can be released, causing the glucose levels to drop dangerously low in times of stress.

Our bones can decrease in density leading to crippling osteoporosis. Heart attacks and stroke can result from a sustained high level of blood clotting chemicals.

Our body's immune system becomes suppressed and we become susceptible to chronic inflammation throughout our bodies. This inflammation can cause heart problems, arthritis, and gastric problems to name a few. Even our ability to think clearly may be impaired.

When we brood over slights and injuries from other people, we can move into a state of mind where resentment becomes habitual. These feelings of dissatisfaction inhibit our responding to life's positive moments. They can cause depression, insomnia, wide emotional mood swings, and explosions of rage which other people may view as irrational.

If you wonder if your resentments have reached a level dangerous to your health, ask yourself how you feel when you plot revenge in an effort to get even with someone.

Do such thoughts lift your mood? Are your plans for revenge detailed and time consuming? If so, your attitude of resentment may be moving toward a habit. Finding a solution for your negative feelings is definitely in order.

Keep in mind that anger and resentment are like muscles. The more you exercise them, the stronger they become. The stronger they become, the more habitual anger and resentment become in your life.

So too, the practice of forgiving.

It is a matter of choice which path you take. It is your decision: health or disease, peace or strife.

"Angry people want you to know
How powerful they are.

Loving people want you to know
How powerful you are."

Chief Red Eagle (William Weatherford)

11

Points to Remember About Anger

"The best fighter is never angry."

--Lao Tzu

Anger is not a primary emotion. It is a feeling that acts as a cover for other more painful emotions such as fear, hurt, or rejection. The feeling of anger keeps a person from feeling vulnerable. The more we depend on anger to protect our feelings, the stronger that dependence becomes and the more we feel we have a right to be angry in emotional situations. This attitude encourages a habit that can be very costly to our relationships and could become physically dangerous in the right situation.

There is a difference between:
- The feeling of anger which is an emotional response to an experience.
- "Acting On" anger which is to use the energy of anger constructively in one's life, such as exercising, working industriously, helping others, painting the house, etc.
- "Acting Out" anger which is an outburst of temper unleashed against other people, creatures, or objects.

"Acting Out" anger:
- Shows that we are out of control.
- Other people may recognize that we are fearful and hurt.
- It is threatening to others, therefore it is abusive.
- It violates the human rights of the people around us.
- Resorting to "acting out" anger is a sign of weakness.
- The more often we "act out" anger, the more we think we need, and have a right, to "act out" our angry feelings.

Coping with the immediate reaction of anger:
- Some people are able to talk immediately about what has angered them and remain calm.
- If you are given to temper outbursts or confusion, leave talking for later.
- If you can't keep your cool, leave the area until you've calmed down.

Dealing with the feelings of anger:

- <u>Acknowledge</u> the feeling of anger. Remember that feelings are neither good nor bad. Feelings are not facts.
- <u>Accept</u> the feeling. Don't fight it. Don't judge it.
- <u>Understand</u> the situation which is stimulating the feeling of anger.

Understanding anger needs a four dimensional approach:

- <u>Physical Dimension</u>: Angry energy needs expending. Use hard exercise, running, pillow pounding or rapid talking preferably to a non-judgmental person who will listen but not comment or share with others later. This is not the time to talk to the person with whom you are angry.
- <u>Emotional Dimension</u>: Talk out your distress with a safe person who won't give advice but will actively listen and help you sort out your disturbed feelings.
- <u>Mental Dimension</u>: Spend some time alone to sift through your thoughts seeking clarity and some understanding of the situation.
- <u>Spiritual Dimension</u>: A positive practice is to spend some time relaxing and meditating until your inner self comes to a place of calmness and peace.

Finally, there is the need to discuss the situation with the offending party if that is possible.

- You need to be fully in charge of yourself when you take this step and approach the discussion without anger.
- Make it clear that you are looking for understanding of the situation so that you can avoid a similar situation in the future. *Understanding what is said to you is not the same as agreeing with what is said.*

If discussion and understanding is not possible, take other actions to find a solution that will bring peace to your mind. You may want to find other employment, make new friends, or invite a loved one to go with you to a professional therapist who might be able to help both of you find a middle ground for discussion and eventual clarity.

"It is easier to leave angry words unspoken
Than to mend a heart those words have broken."

Author Unknown

APPENDICES

Appendix #1

Information on Those Quoted

Andy Andrews, 5/22/1959, NY Times Bestselling Christian American Author and Corporate Speaker. Authored *"The Heart Mender"* in 2010.

Sir Francis Bacon, 1/22/1561—4/9/1626, English Philosopher, Jurist, Statesman, Scientist, Author, Orator, called the Creator of Empiricism, Advocate of the Scientific Method during the Scientific Revolution, Knighted in 1603.

Ambrose Bierce, 6/24/1841—1914, American Editorialist, Journalist, Short Story Writer and Satirist, wrote "An Occurrence at Owl Creek" and "The Devil's Dictionary."

Chief Red Eagle, 1780—1824, identified himself as a "Creek Warrior," Also known as William Weatherford. Brilliant War Strategist, fought Andrew Jackson's army. Jackson's comment about him was, "He is fit to command armies."

Confucius, 551—479 BC, Chinese Philosopher, Founder of the Ru School of Chinese Thought.

Alexandre Dumas, 7/24/1802—12/5/1870, French Playwright and Writer of historical novels which have been translated into 100 languages, including *"The Three Musketeers"* (1844), and *"The Count of Monte Cristo"* (1845-46).

Sidharthma Gautama, Buddha, 6th Century BC, his doctrines became the foundation of Buddhism. Authored "Dhammapada."

Viktor E. Frankl, MD, PhD, 3/26/1905—9/2/1997, Austrian Neurologist, Psychiatrist, and Holocaust Survivor. Founder of Logo-therapy, a form of existential analysis, the Third Viennese School of Psychotherapy, Author of *"Man's Search for Meaning."*

Emma Goldman, 6/27/1869—5/14/1940, Atheist, born in Russia to Orthodox Jewish Family, moved to New York in 1885, died in Canada. Anarchist Political Philosopher, Writer, Lecturer regarding women's rights and social issues. Founded *"Mother Earth"* Journal in 1906. Jailed repeatedly in New York regarding social issues and implicated in the attempted murder of Henry Clay Fisk. After two years in jail, she was deported back to Russia in 1919. She lived in many countries thereafter.

Criss Jami, 5/29/1987, (Christopher James Gilbert), American Existentialist Philosopher, Poet, and Lead Singer of the Rock Band "Venus in Arms," Authored *Salome'* in 2011.

Martin Luther King, Jr., 1/15/1929—4/4/1968, American Baptist Minister, Humanitarian, African-American Civil Rights Leader, Assassinated.

Ann Lamott, 4/10/1954, American Christian Novelist and Non-Fiction Writer, Progressive Political Activist, Public Speaker, Writing Teacher, Called the "People's Author" because of the documentary on her life, *"Birds"* and her social media activities. Saw books as medicine.

Stephen Levine, 7/17/1987, American Poet, Author, and Buddhist Teacher who alludes to the Creator as God, The Beloved, The One, marking a difference between his teachings and the teachings of other Buddhist Leaders. Uses meditation in his work with the sick and dying. Authored *"A Year to Live,"* 1998.

Allan Lokos, 1941, Interfaith Minister and Teacher, Founder and Director of the Community Meditation Center in New York City. Studied under the Dalai Lama, Authored *"Patience: The Art of Peaceful Living,"* 2012.

Nelson Mandela, 7/8/1918—12/5/2013, South African Anti-Apartheid Revolutionary, Moral and Political Leader, Journalist, jailed for 27 years for his leadership, became first black President of South Africa.

Jude Morgan, (Tim Wilson) The United Kingdom Historical Fiction Writers, Authored "*Indiscretion*," 2005.

Lance Morrow, 9/21/1939, Roman Catholic, Author, Essayist, Columnist chiefly for Time Magazine. Former Professor of Journalism at Boston University, Authored "*The Chief*," 1985.

Mike Norton, 7/31/1988, American Author, US Military Veteran, 7 time Winner of the USS Dwight Eisenhower Award for essays of World Peace and Respect, Authored "*Fighting for Redemption*," 2011.

Stephen Richards, Author and Clinical Hypnotherapist, Previous Member British Association of Counsellors, Authored "*Forgiveness and Love Conquers All*," 2011.

Eleanor Roosevelt, 10/11/1884—11/7/1962, Human Rights Activist, Columnist, On Gallop's List of Most Widely Admired People of the 20th Century, First Lady of the United States 1933-1945, First Chair of United Nations Committee on Human Rights, Delegate to the United Nations, Influential on the Universal Declaration of Human Rights, Chaired John F. Kennedy's Presidential Commission on the Status of Women. Active in Civil Rights of African-Americans, Asians, World War II refugees, and Women in the Work Place.

Jalal ad Muhammad Rumi, 9/30/1207—12/17/1273, Considered a great Muslim Saint, Persian Poet, Jurist, Islamic Scholar, Theologian, Sufi Mystic, a Best-selling Poet in the US (per Christian Science Monitor, 11/25/1997). Born in Tajikistan, Buried in Turkey

G. Bernard Shaw, 7/26/1856—11/2/1950, Born in Dublin, Ireland, co-founder of London School of Economics, Orator, Social Propagandist, Playwright, Theatre Critic for Saturday Review, Won Nobel Prize for Literature in 1925, and an Academy Award in 1938 for his play "Pygmalion" (1913) which became "My Fair Lady" in 1956.

Lewis B. Smedes, 8/20/1921—12/19/2002, Christian Author, Ethicist and Theologian in the Reformed Tradition, Professor of Theology and Ethics for 25 years at Fuller Theological Seminary, Pasadena, Calif. Also taught at the Free University in Amsterdam and Calvin College in Grand Rapids, Mich. Authored "*Forgive and Forget*," 1984.

Socrates, 469—399 BC, Greek Philosopher, Teacher and esteemed Wise Man throughout the ages.

Andrew Solomon, 10/30/1963, dual citizen of New York and London, Writer on Politics, Culture and Psychology, His Book, "*The Noonday Demon*" won the 2001 National Book Award, was a finalist for 2002 Pulitzer Prize and was included in The Times list of 100 best books of the decade.

Thomas Stephen Szasz, (pronounced Sass) 4/15/1920—9/18/2012 American Psychiatrist and Libertarian, Professor of Psychiatry at State University of New York Upstate Medical Union, named Humanist of the Year in 1973 by the American Humanist Assoc. Born to Jewish parents in Budapest, Hungary.

Lao Tzu, 604 BC—531 BC, China, Philosopher and Poet, "author of Tao Tu Ching and founder of philosophical Taoism, Revered as a Deity in religious Taoism and other Chinese religions.

William Paul Young, 5/11/1955, Canadian Author, born to Missionary Parents living in New Guina, learned the language and culture of the stone age tribal people, the Dani, Devotee of C.S.Lewis, his book "*The Shack*" was a NY Times Best Seller.

Appendix #2

Additional Helpful Resources

Don't Grow Old – Grow Up! Dorothy Carnegie, E.P. Dutton, NY, 1984

Help for Shy People, Gerald M. Phillips, Prentice-Hall, Inc., NJ 1986

How to Get Going When You Can Barely Get Out of Bed, Linda J. Bailey, Prentice Hall, NJ, 1984

How to Win Friends and Influence People, Dale Carnegie, Read the book or take a class available in most cities, Pocket Books, 1998

Learned Optimism, How to Change Your Mind and Your Life, Martin E. P. Seligman, PhD, Simon & Schuster, 2011

Lighten Up! The Amazing Power of Grace Under Pressure, C. W. Metcalf, Nightingale-Conant Corp. 1994

The Secret Strength in Depression, 3rd Ed., Frederick Flack, MD, Hatherleigh Press, 2002

Man's Search for Meaning, 1st Ed. 1946, Simon & Schuster's Pocket Books, last printing in 2014.

When I say NO, I Feel Guilty, Manuel J. Smith, PhD., Bantam Books, 2011

Your Perfect Right: Assertiveness & Equality in Your Life and Relationships, 9th Ed., Robert L. Alberti and Michael L. Emmons 2008

Made in the USA
Charleston, SC
29 April 2015